Measuring and Evaluating

Module 4

ASTD Press is an internationally renowned source of insightful and practical information on workplace learning and performance topics, including training basics, evaluation and return-on-investment (ROI), instructional systems development (ISD), e-learning, leadership, and career development.

Ordering information: This ASTD Learning System and other books published by ASTD Press can be purchased by visiting our website at store.astd.org or by calling 800.628.2783 or 703.683.8100.

Library of Congress Control Number: 2006920959

ISBN-13: 987-1-56286-442-2
ISBN-10: 1-56286-442-4

ASTD Press Staff
Director: Cat Russo
Manager: Mark Morrow
Associate Editor: Tora Estep
Associate Editor: Jennifer Mitchell
Circulation Manager: Marnee Beck
Editorial Assistant: Kelly Norris
Bookstore and Inventory: Nancy Silva
Marketing Manager: Greg Akroyd
Production Coordinator: Rachel Beuter
Cover Design: Alizah Epstein

Printed by Victor Graphics, Baltimore, Maryland, www.victorgraphics.com.

Table of Contents

Note: To ensure optimal instructional design in this module, the order of some Key Knowledge areas has been changed from the *Early Bird Guide to ASTD Professional Certification* (2005). These changes do not affect the integrity of the content.

1
Theories and Types of Evaluation

Everyone knows the lingo: reengineering, downsizing, rightsizing, competition, globalization—the list seems endless. What these terms represent is the accelerated climate of change in organizations. Faced with maturing markets and global competition, leadership in the corporate, non-profit, and government sectors has become extremely demanding in its analysis of existing business processes and procedures and overall organizational health.

One aspect of this introspection is the desire to eliminate waste and redundancy. Corporate overhead—or support functions not directly responsible for generating revenue—have come under increased scrutiny. The support functions that have survived this scrutiny best are those that learned, early on, how to operate like independent businesses—providing optimal customer service while emphasizing value for the dollars spent. Measuring and evaluating are essential skills that allow workplace learning and performance professionals to show the relevance of learning to organizational goals and strategies.

To produce meaningful information about value, the measurement and evaluation process should be designed and conducted systematically. Knowledge of formal approaches to evaluation enables practitioners to develop models that are appropriate for their particular applications and to communicate those models to stakeholders, to ensure that results inform decision making effectively.

Learning Objectives:

- ☑ Define and list the purpose and benefits of training evaluation.
- ☑ Outline the five key steps in the measurement process.
- ☑ Discuss assessment development issues, including reliability and validity.
- ☑ Define the use of Tyler's goal attainment model as it relates to measurement and evaluation.
- ☑ Differentiate between Scriven's formative and summative evaluation and list the three types of formative evaluations.
- ☑ Describe the four levels of Kirkpatrick's evaluation method and give examples for each.
- ☑ Describe the return-on-investment (ROI) methodology and its purpose.
- ☑ Review and illustrate the components of the balanced scorecard approach to measurement and evaluation.
- ☑ Define meta-evaluation and describe its use in the project management of evaluation.

Purpose and Benefits of Training Evaluation

Leading-edge training and development organizations, whether through internal staff or contractors providing services, know that their success depends on demonstrating the value of training investment. The simplest way to prove training's value to a client is to document that the training has achieved its desired outcome—through evaluation.

Evaluation methods help determine whether training achieves its objectives. Programs that are structured and designed properly have objectives or elements that specify what the training must accomplish and in what time period these accomplishments must be realized.

Herein lies the fundamental secret of evaluating training: The evaluation process and procedure must be incorporated at the start, and it must be an integral part of any program development process. For example, baseline data must be collected before training begins; otherwise, there's no basis for any meaningful comparison with training program results. Historically, evaluation of training has been done after training rather than before and after. If program development follows the classic steps of assessing needs and generating objectives, the evaluation criteria that follow are then based on measuring how well the program components—students, instructors, and materials—have met these objectives and answered these questions.

A sound system of evaluating training provides valuable information for the learner, client, training management, and senior corporate management. The information elicited from training evaluations should be the final instrument on which training decisions, such as program additions, changes, or deletions, should be made. Good evaluations document the results of training programs, which can be used subsequently to prioritize training needs at the organizational level. Then financial and other resources can be shifted from training that has less impact on corporate goals to those objectives that have the most favorable cost-benefit ratio.

These are some benefits of evaluation:

- *Determining business impact, the cost-benefit ratio, and the ROI for the program:* What was the shift in the identified business metric? What part of the shift was attributable to the learning experience? Was the benefit to the organization worth the total cost of providing the learning experience? What is the bottom-line value of the course's impact on the organization?

- *Improving the design of the learning experience:* Evaluation can help verify the needs assessment, learning objectives, instructional strategies, target audience, delivery method, and quality of delivery and course content.

- *Determining whether the objectives of the learning experience were met and to what extent:* The objectives are stated in measurable and specific terms. Evaluation determines whether each stated objective was met. Nevertheless, knowing only whether objectives were met isn't enough; a practitioner must know the *extent* to which objectives were met. This knowledge helps focus future efforts for content reinforcement and improvement.

- *Determining the content's adequacy:* How can the content be more job related? Was the content too advanced or not challenging enough? Does all the content support the learning objectives?

- *Assessing the effectiveness and appropriateness of instructional strategies:* Case studies, tests, exercises, and other instructional strategies must be relevant to the job and reinforce course content. Does the instructional strategy link to a course objective and the course content? Is it the right instructional strategy to drive the desired learning or practice? Was there enough instruction and feedback? Does the strategy fit with the organization's culture? Instructional strategies, when used as part of evaluation, measure the knowledge, skills, and attitudes the learning experience offers.

- *Reinforcing learning:* Some evaluation methods can reinforce learning. For example, a test or similar performance assessment can focus on content to measure and evaluate content retention. The measurement process itself causes learners to reflect on the content, select the appropriate content area, and use it in the evaluation process.

- *Providing feedback to the facilitator:* Did the facilitator know the content? Did the facilitator stay on topic? Did the facilitator provide added depth and value based on personal experience? Was the facilitator credible? Will the evaluation information be used to improve the facilitator's skills?

- *Determining the appropriate pace and sequence:* Does the practitioner need to schedule more or less time for the total learning experience or certain parts of the learning? Were some parts of the learning experience covered too fast or too slowly? Does the flow of the content make sense? Does the sequence follow a building-block approach?

- *Providing feedback to participants about their learning:* Are participants learning the course content? Which parts are they not learning? Was there a shift in knowledge and skills? To what extent can participants demonstrate the desired skills or behavior?

- *Identifying which participants are experiencing success in the learning program:* Evaluation can identify which participants are grasping the new knowledge and skills and which are struggling. Likewise, evaluation can identify participants who are excelling at understanding the content and using on the job.

- *Identifying the learning being used on the job:* What parts of the learning experience are being used on the job? To what extent are they being used?

- *Assessing the on-the-job environment to support learning:* What environmental factors support or inhibit the use of the new knowledge, skills, attitudes, and behaviors on the job? These factors could be management support, tools and equipment, recognition and reward, and so on.

Although this list is not exhaustive, it does highlight some key purposes of evaluation.

Performance Agreement Principle

Every learning objective should have a corresponding evaluation task. Some evaluation tasks are formal, others are informal. Formal evaluation tasks include taking tests or quizzes and writing an essay. Informal evaluation tasks might include having a learner describe a concept or principle or state a corporate regulation.

Objectives should match evaluation tasks closely in two important areas: behavior and condition. Behavior describes the anticipated outcome of the training (for example, "be able to accurately describe the four components of a widget"), while condition describes the circumstances under which performance is to take place (for example, "given a job aid that describes the four components"). When these elements match, an objective is said to have a performance agreement. The performance agreement principle ensures consistency between what's expected of learners in the objective and what they're required to do in an evaluation.

Benefits of Evaluation

Evaluating learning experiences confers several advantages to the human resource development (HRD) function and to the organization. First, an effective, high-quality evaluation can secure client support and build client relationships. Discussing the evaluation plan demonstrates that the practitioner has a structured approach to ensure quality and continuous improvement of training efforts. This approach gives clients confidence that their investment is well placed.

Second, and in concert with the first benefit, evaluation allows the practitioner to see whether the results of learning are consistent with the business opportunity analysis and needs assessment. What contribution did training make to the shift in the business metric? What was the organizational impact?

Third, evaluation helps focus the training. Is the practitioner using the right content, is it directed to the right audience, and was it delivered effectively? The evaluation results provide information about the target audience and each participant. Evaluation also assesses alignment of the content with learning objectives, needs assessment data, and instructional strategies.

Fourth, evaluation validates performance gaps and learner needs. Through various performance measurements (tests, behavioral checklists, action planning, and so forth), a practitioner can identify ongoing needs. If a learner can't perform a skill or pass a test, a gap still exists that needs to be addressed.

Fifth, evaluation can help determine whether training is the solution to a performance gap. Training is generally part of the solution if

- a shift in the business metric occurred

- participants learned and can apply their new knowledge and skills

- the original problem or opportunity was addressed.

Evaluation can also determine whether the program was a cost-effective solution. By knowing the total costs of the learning experience and the dollar value of the benefit (from the shift in the business metric), practitioners can determine the ROI. Obviously, positive ROI is desirable.

Sixth, if practitioners can demonstrate value, they may gain access to more resources. Management will fund initiatives that make a difference to it and the organization. By helping management meet its objectives, practitioners become a partner in that success.

Measurement Process

A broad range of methods and tools are available for every evaluation approach. Options include direct observation, comparisons of tests taken before and after training, interviews, reports, follow-up tests, questionnaires, and surveys. The most effective approach includes combinations of these methods. Depending on the objectives, the nature of the training, the characteristics of the learners, and the focus of the evaluation, some methods are more appropriate than others.

All evaluation models contain the following steps:

- identifying evaluation goals

- developing an evaluation design and strategy

- selecting and constructing measurement tools

- analyzing data

- reporting data.

Incorporating evaluation measures into the training design from the onset is essential, and making sure they are kept simple is important. The value being created for the organization must be monitored continually throughout the program after the evaluation's benefits have been "sold" to the appropriate user. During the measurement process, the evaluator should keep a watchful eye on execution and progress.

Evaluation Development Issues: Validity and Reliability

Two terms that are heard frequently in evaluation circles are *validity* and *reliability*. When reporting the results of an evaluation, practitioners may be asked how they know the data is valid or the measures are reliable. Knowing these terms helps them respond intelligently. More important, understanding these concepts can help practitioners construct better evaluation instruments, such as questionnaires and tests.

Validity

Validity means measuring what the practitioner intended to measure. For example, if a group of e-learning participants misinterpret the intended meaning of a test question, the resulting data would not be valid. Verifying the validity of an evaluation instrument can involve complex statistical intervention. Without the assistance of a statistician, the most practical way to improve the validity of evaluation instruments is to solicit feedback from subject matter experts (SMEs). A practitioner should ask SMEs and participants to review each question with a critical eye and then administer the instrument to test subjects and compare their test results and perceptions of the question meaning with the intended meaning.

Types of Validity

For data collection information to be valid and reliable, sound development and use of the instruments are the practitioners challenge. According to Jack Phillips (1998), there are five ways to determine whether an instrument is valid:

- *Content validity* is the extent to which the instrument represents the program's content is content validity. Low-content validity means the instrument doesn't represent a true summation of the program content. High-content validity means the instrument represents a good balance of all the program content.

- *Construct validity* is the degree to which an instrument represents the construct it's supposed to measure. The abstract variable that the instrument is intended to measure, such as the skill or ability, is the construct. Construct validity can be defended through expert opinion, correlations, logical deductions, and criterion group studies.

- *Concurrent validity* is the extent to which an instrument agrees with the results of other instruments administered at approximately the same time to measure the same characteristics.

- *Criterion validity* is the extent to which the assessment can predict or agree with external constructs. Criterion validity is determined by looking at the correlation between the instrument and the criterion measure.

- *Predictive validity* is the extent to which an instrument can predict future behaviors or results.

Reliability

Reliability refers to the ability of the same measurement to produce consistent results over time. Certain types of data are inherently reliable, such as a person's age. When evaluating this type of data, practitioners can feel confident that they will get reliable results every time. Other more subjective types of data can be much less reliable. Scientifically determining an instrument's reliability requires that it be administered to a sample of participants and undergo statistical analysis. Without scientific intervention, practitioners can still attempt to improve reliability by considering the types of data they're trying to measure and wording questions carefully to increase the likelihood that participants consistently respond in the same manner. Practitioners can also assess consistency by evaluating responses over time, although just because an instrument produces results over time does not necessarily mean that it's valid. It could be measuring the wrong thing but doing it consistently.

The Relationship of Reliability to Validity

To arrive at test validity, a practitioner should evaluate the degree to which guesswork (which is sometimes necessary) supports conclusions and actions. Whether an evaluation is accurate is determined by weighting the overall test scores or other modes of assessment with the more speculative components of the evaluation.

Reliability refers to the consistency of measurement and can be interpreted as an index of test results error. Generally, tests with reliability coefficients at or above 75 percent ($p=0.75$) are considered adequate.

Test validity determines that a test accurately measures what it's intended to measure, and test reliability determines how frequently it succeeds. Both indexes are used to determine whether inferences and actions based on test scores are on target.

Test validity incorporates several aspects of the testing process into a single judgment—whether the test is or is not valid. This judgment should be based on several test result aspects, including these two considerations:

- Is the test reasonably reliable (for example, free from significant measurement errors)?

- Does the test content sufficiently cover the material presented in the training program that is needed to perform the job safely and competently? Information on test content is often based on expert judgment and involves SME assessment of individual items. Item analysis can help guide this process, but it can't take the place of true expert evaluation of item content.

Neil Salkind (2005) outlines this relationship in the following way: If validity and reliability were targets on a dartboard, validity would be the bull's eye. If the measure hits the bull's eye, it is valid; if it hits the bull's eye every time, it is valid and reliable. Just as important, however, if the measure consistently hits some other segment on the board, it's still reliable; however, it's not valid because it missed the bull's eye. Although a measure can be reliable and not valid, it can't be valid without being reliable. Validity is concerned with what's being measured; reliability is concerned with how consistently the measure is measuring what it's intended to measure.

Test Difficulty

Test reliability and validity are maximized if the level of difficulty for answering most test items is more than just a chance possibility and, at the same time, the degree of difficulty is not too high. If a test is too easy, it shows up in overall high grade averages, which in turn translate into poor job performance, on-the-job accidents, or damage to expensive equipment. If a test is too difficult, it becomes apparent if overall grade averages are low.

A test or test question that appears to be on the easy side could mean the information was well taught, answers were cued in some way, or participants already knew the information. When it becomes apparent that a test or test item is too difficult, perhaps it wasn't presented adequately in the training session or in reading materials, or maybe the item is so difficult that only the most knowledgeable participants are able to answer it correctly.

Split-Half Check of Reliability

Split-half is a type of test reliability in which one test is split into two shorter ones. It's achieved by assigning test items randomly to one test half or the other. Each half is scored, and the correlation between the halves is calculated to provide a measure of response and consistency. The participants retest with the unused half, which overcomes the memory bias in a test–retest approach.

Test–Retest Check of Reliability

The test–retest approach does just what the name implies: The same test is administered twice to the same group of people, and the scores are compared. Memory can play a factor. With too short a period between tests, a participant could simply remember the questions. With too long a period, other variables, such as exposure to new information, enter the equation. Timing is the critical issue in a test–retest check of reliability.

Goal Attainment Methods and Performance-Based Training Evaluation

In 1949, Ralph W. Tyler synthesized the basic concepts of goal attainment for instruction. In Tyler's model, "objectives, the ends of instruction, are first identified. The content of instruction is identified to address the objectives, and the various instructional elements, the means, are then designed to assist learners in obtaining the objectives" (Herschbach 1992).

Tyler's model poses these four questions:

- What objectives should learners achieve?
- What learning activities will assist learners to achieve these objectives?
- How should the curriculum be organized?
- How should learner achievement be evaluated?

Another approach to evaluation, similar to Tyler's, is the performance-based training (PBT) model that Marshall and Schriver (1994) developed. PBT requires that a learner demonstrate both knowledge and skills before leaving training. The following model, which is similar to PBT, is used to separate knowledge and skills. Its five levels include:

1. *Self:* A practitioner needs feedback. Practitioners often overlook the need to conduct self-analysis feedback but should take time to reflect on performance

and to ask what went well, what didn't go so well, and what might need to change. In addition to their own insights, practitioners can receive feedback from trainees' evaluation forms and colleagues' feedback.

2. *Course materials:* The materials are usually designed in a one-dimensional written format. It's impossible to know how the written notes and suggested processes are going to evolve until the training takes place. Therefore, the learners' comments, written trainees' evaluation critiques, and the practitioner's observations in the training session provide the needed feedback. Questions might include: Does the material work? Are some portions difficult to deliver? Do learners exhibit difficulty with materials or training situations? Do courses or training processes need revising or updating?

3. *Course curriculum:* The implementation phase of course design allows a practitioner to test the design by getting feedback during the training delivery process. Feedback would, therefore, come from the practitioner, learners, or observers. Questions might include: Does the course curriculum hang together? Does the course meet the intended learning objectives and outcomes?

4. *Course modules:* As with course materials and course design, course modules are a written interpretation of what the practitioner should deliver. Feedback consists of a self-analysis of course modules, the practitioner's experience during the delivery stage, and reactions from learners or observers. Questions might include: Are the modules organized around a theme? Are the topics sequenced in logical order? Does each module contribute to the course outcomes and learning objectives?

5. *Learning transfer:* Both written and oral feedback about the transfer of learning to the workplace is important during the training event and as a posttraining activity. Questions might include: How effective was the transfer of skills and knowledge to each learner's work situation? How effective has the learning been implemented in the real world of work?

Output Models

There are two categories of evaluation, each providing different information to ensure that the training is on track:

- *Program evaluation* assesses the impact of a training program on learning.

- *Training transfer evaluation* measures the success of the learner's ability to transfer the learning back on the job.

Wholey, Hatry, and Newcomer (2004) describe program evaluation as the systematic assessment of program results and, to the extent feasible, systematic assessment of the extent to which the program caused those results. Evaluation includes ongoing monitoring of programs as well as one-shot studies of program processes or program impact. The approaches used are based on social science research methodologies and professional standards. A program is a set of resources and activities directed toward one or more common goals, typically under the direction of a single manager or management team. A program may consist of a limited set of activities in one agency (or organization) or a complex set of activities implemented at many sites to two or more levels in an organization and by a set of public, nonprofit, and even private providers.

Formative Versus Summative Evaluation

One of the key challenges of preparing a training program is making sure it actually accomplishes the objectives for which it was developed. Michael Scriven first proposed the difference between summative and formative program evaluation in 1967. These two terms were applied to assessment and evaluation processes for measuring a training program's effectiveness by Benjamin Bloom, Thomas Hastings, and George Madaus (1971) in *Handbook of Formative and Summative Evaluation of Student Learning*.

Assessing the effectiveness of a training program while it's under development is called *formative evaluation* because the assessment is done while the training program is being formed. *Summative evaluation* assesses the effectiveness of a training program that's already generally available, such as a classroom course listed in a course catalog and available for enrollment or a workbook that learners can order and use immediately.

The sole purpose of formative evaluation is to improve the draft training program and increase the likelihood that it will achieve its objectives when it's made generally available. A practitioner should conduct a formative evaluation while the training program is under development and, instead of reporting results externally, use this information to revise the training program immediately and make it more effective upon general availability.

Specifically, during formative evaluation, a practitioner should try to make sure the training program is

- *Understandable:* Learners should be able to comprehend content on the first explanation and follow exercises with no additional assistance besides that supplied in the instructions. Learners should not be slowed by inconsistencies in content or terminology, by grammatical errors, or by awkwardly presented content.

- *Accurate:* The material should be current and correct. Addresses of websites shown to the class should be accurate and working.

- *Functional:* Printed pages should match those onscreen in word processors. Slides should appear on the projector as they do on the computer screen. Hands-on exercises should work as intended.

Three Types of Formative Evaluation

To make sure a course is understandable, accurate, and functional, practitioners conduct three types of formative evaluation:

- *Pilot tests:* For these evaluations, a practitioner conducts the training program for the first time with people who represent the intended learners for the purpose of assessing which parts work and which ones need improvement.

- *Technical reviews:* For these evaluations, SMEs verify the accuracy of the content.

- *Production reviews:* For these evaluations, editors assess the completeness and style of the content, and production specialists make sure the printed and projected output matches what appears on the computer screen.

Donald Kirkpatrick's Four Levels of Evaluation

Transfer of training is the effective and continuing on-the-job application of knowledge and skills gained in training—both on and off the job. Although learning is the planned outcome of any training solution, the most appropriate critical event for any training intervention is to have the learner transfer new skills, knowledge, and abilities to the job.

Learning transfer can occur in a variety of ways. Donald L. Kirkpatrick developed one of the most popular models. In his book *Evaluating Training Programs: The Four Levels,* 2nd edition, Kirkpatrick identifies the following four levels at which training can be evaluated:

- *Level 1: Reaction* measures attitude or feeling regarding satisfaction and dissatisfaction with the training.

- *Level 2: Learning* measures observable or measurable behavior change in the classroom or training situation.

- *Level 3: Behavior* measures new or changed behavior and performance back on the job.

- *Level 4: Results* measures, for example, increased productivity; sales quality; or reduction in costs, accidents, and grievances caused by appropriate training that addressed the identified need.

Level 1 evaluates a learner's reaction. Reaction sheets, also known as happy sheets or smile sheets, are the most popular mechanism for conducting this evaluation. This evaluation measures only how a person feels about the training—that is, happy or not happy. Usually these sheets are distributed at the end of a training session. Level 1 feedback may also include word-of-mouth feedback to the instructor, managers, or other employees about how much a participant enjoyed a session.

Level 2 evaluates a learner's mastery of the program content by using a test to determine participants' ability to demonstrate the knowledge or skills. This evaluation measures only the learner's ability to answer test questions.

Level 3 evaluates a learner's ability to transfer the learning on the job and the degree to which participants have applied the training or knowledge to their jobs. This evaluation is difficult to accomplish unless the practitioner has had previous discussions with the learner's supervisor or manager, and they agreed that certain mastery should occur in learning and the successful transfer of the training will be reported back.

Level 4 evaluates the training's organizational impact. This evaluation can be accomplished only if a well-defined training need that affected the organization was identified and training targeted the issue. Level 4 seeks to measure the quantifiable changes in key performance measures. When measuring the organizational impact, some factors and types of data to consider include

- difficulty in isolating effects of the intervention in comparison with other factors affecting the result-control groups

- types of evaluation

- productivity and production measures as benchmarks

- cost or expense measurements

- sales results

- management support

- other financial or direct output measures

- employee performance in quality, quantity, and ability to follow processes

- organization culture barriers and enablers

- department performance

- employee turnover

- customer satisfaction ratings on products and services.

How does a practitioner get from the four levels of evaluation to designing and conducting the course? Table 1-1 shows each of Kirkpatrick's levels and when to measure, what to measure, and how to measure for successful learning transfer. The premise of Kirkpatrick's evaluation model is that these four levels can be used to design and test how successful the practitioner was in presenting information for the learner to master. Practitioners, however, can manage and test successful transfer only at Levels 1 and 2. After they begin to assess the success of learning transfer at Level 3, they must include the learner's supervisor or manager, or both, back on the job.

Practitioners must be aware that positive results from Levels 1 through 3 don't ensure that training will have an impact on all bottom-line business results. When practitioners want to test the level of successful transfer at Level 4, results, they must start with a well-defined needs assessment statement, which specifies a need that has a significant impact on the organization and shows training as the solution to the defined need. After the training has occurred, they can test to determine the impact training had on that need.

Table 1-1. Evaluation Worksheet

Level	When to Measure	What to Measure	Instrument Used
1	• During the program (end of day) • End of program	• Reactions • Pace and sequence • Relevance (content) • Instrument strategies • Interaction • Facilitators' style • Level of discussion • Objectives met • Environment • Knowledge of facilitator • Participant interaction • Registration process	• Questionnaire • Individual responses in class • Follow-up interviews • Observation checklists
2	• During the program • Before the program • After the program	• learning and extent of learning • Teaching of content • Knowledge of participants	• Knowledge tests, which may be paper-and-pencil tests; oral questions and answers • Performance tests, role plays, case studies with evaluation or feedback sheets • Monitored skill demonstrations • Checklists • Product tests
3	• After the program • A few weeks to three months	• On-the-job change	• Performance records • Performance contracts • Action plans • Interviews • Direct observation with checklists • Supervisor interviews
4	• After the program • Three months to one year	• Impact on organization	• Action plans • Interviews • Questionnaires • Focus groups • Performance contracts

Phillip's ROI Methodology

Donald Kirkpatrick's four levels of evaluation have become a framework for many practitioners. HRD staff must conduct, in addition to the established evaluations, another measurement: ROI. According to Jack Phillips, the issue of ROI in training and development has become a critical challenge for HRD personnel. In the past decade, the interest in ROI has mushroomed, leaving most major organizations scrambling for ways to tackle the issue.

In response to this interest, Phillips added ROI as the fifth level to the four-level evaluation framework. This fifth level represents steps in cost-benefit analysis and begins with converting improvement in Level 4 measures to monetary value. The techniques include the use of

- standard values, which is the most credible approach given that standard values are ones that are already accepted in the organization

- historical costs, which represent what the measures being converted have cost the organization in the past (such as the cost of an unexpected absence)

- expert input, using input from internal or external experts on a particular measure

- participant estimates, an undervalued source of data, but a conservative process can provide accurate and credible data

- linking measures to other measures that have already been converted, a technique used in many organizations when placing value on customer and employee satisfaction (Sasser, Schlesinger, and Heskett 1997)

- supervisor and manager estimates, using the same techniques as participant estimates, but participants are the more credible source

- learning staff estimates, which are the least credible source for data conversion.

Table 1-2 shows Level 5 evaluation and when to measure, what to measure, and how to measure for successful learning transfer.

Table 1-2. ROI Worksheet

Level	When to Measure	What to Measure	Instrument Used
5	<ul><li>After program</li><li>Three months to one year</li></ul>	<ul><li>Monetary value of impact</li></ul>	<ul><li>Control groups</li><li>Trend line</li><li>Participants' estimates</li><li>Supervisors' estimates</li><li>Managements' estimates</li><li>Use of experts</li><li>Extant data</li><li>External studies</li></ul>

Along with adding a fifth level of evaluation, the ROI methodology includes a critical step to isolate the effects of training, which answers the question "How do we know it was our training that caused the results?" The answer is often found by using a control group arrangement, but sometimes this approach isn't feasible for a variety of reasons. Some approaches for isolating the effects of training are

- use of control groups

- trend line analysis

- forecasting methods

- participant's estimate of impact (percent)

- supervisor's estimate of impact (percent)

- management's estimate of impact (percent)

- use of experts

- subordinate's report of other factors

- calculating or estimating the impact of other factors

- customer input.

The ROI methodology also includes a process model with a step-by-step formula for developing data categorized in the five-level framework and guiding principles that ensure consistent application.

ROI has become a hot topic for some good reasons:

- In most industrialized nations, HRD budgets have continued to grow year after year, and as expenditures grow, accountability becomes a more critical issue. An increasing budget draws the attention of internal critics, often forcing the development of ROI.

- Total quality management and continuous process improvement have focused increased attention on measurement issues.

- The reengineering and restructuring experience and the increase in outsourcing has caused many HRD executives to focus on bottom-line issues.

- The business management mindset of current training and HRD managers leads them to place more emphasis on economic issues within the training function.

- Accountability has been a persistent trend for all functions in organizations.

- Top executives are demanding ROI calculations in organizations where they weren't required previously.

To calculate ROI, practitioners convert Level 4 data to monetary values and compare with program costs. This conversion requires placing a value on each unit of data connected with the program. A number of techniques are available to convert data to monetary values; the selection depends on the type of data and the situation.

To measure how well trainees absorbed material covered in the training program, a practitioner should take advantage of a variety of assessment tools. Among the most common and effective assessment methods are checklists, questionnaires, and interviews. Checklists allow practitioners or facilitators, managers, and trainees to assign value to different training topics. The disadvantage of checklists is that answers are subjective, so they are not necessarily valid.

The Balanced Scorecard Approach

Using a balanced scorecard is a way for organizations to evaluate effectiveness beyond using only financial measures (Kaplan and Norton 1996). This model consists of measuring effectiveness by using four perspectives:

- *The customer perspective:* Did the solution, intervention, or practice meet the customer's need or expectation?

- *The innovation and learning perspective:* Did users gain the needed skills or knowledge?

- *The internal business perspective:* Did the solution, intervention, or practice have an effect back on the job?

- *The financial perspective:* Did the solution, intervention, or practice have a financial payoff?

Although at first glance these four perspectives seem similar to Kirkpatrick's levels of evaluation, the balanced scorecard approach looks at an entire organization, not just training and development.

Meta-Evaluation Methods

Meta evaluation is an evaluation of an evaluation. According to David J. Basarab and Darrell K. Root (1992) in their book *The Training Evaluation Process,* "These evaluations are conducted to provide assurances of the quality of an evaluation, to provide, when necessary, credibility to the evaluation, and to improve subsequent evaluations." During the project management phase of an evaluation program, a practitioner should analyze each step to evaluate the evaluation. Project management of evaluation is best when a project plan is in place to direct and control the project, and when needed resources are organized, staffed, and assigned to specific tasks. Project management includes

- strategic human resource performance
- performance improvement plans and processes
- program effectiveness
- monitoring and control of the project
- planning of the evaluation in terms of tasks, timeframes, roles, and constraints.

Evaluation Instruments

Paper-and-pencil tests: This method measures how well trainees learn program content. An instructor administers paper-and-pencil tests in class to measure participants' progress.

E-learning tests: Like paper-and-pencil tests, this method measures how well learners learn program content. E-learning tests are embedded in e-learning programs.

Opinion surveys: Opinion surveys determine what changes in attitude have occurred as a result of training. Practitioners use these surveys to gather information about employees' perceptions, work habits, motivations, value beliefs, work relations, and so on. Attitude surveys also reveal respondents' opinions about their jobs, the workplace, co-workers, supervisors, policies, procedures, and the organization.

Simulations and on-site observations: Instructors' or managers' observations of on-the-job performance in a work simulation indicate whether learners' skills have improved as a result of the training.

Productivity reports: Hard production data, such as sales reports and manufacturing totals, can help managers and instructors determine *actual* performance improvement on the job.

Pretraining surveys: Pretraining surveys are used to identify training needs and learner attitudes toward training.

Posttraining surveys: Progress and proficiency assessments by both managers and participants indicate perceived performance improvement on the job. Attitudes are also often measured on posttraining surveys.

Needs, objectives, and content comparisons: Training managers, participants, and supervisors compare needs analysis results with course objectives and content to determine whether the program was relevant to participants' needs. Relevancy ratings at the end of the program also contribute to the comparison.

Evaluation forms: Participants' responses on end-of-program evaluation forms indicate what they liked and disliked about the training.

Professional opinions: Instructional designers critique and assess the quality of the program design.

Instructor evaluations: Professional practitioners administer assessment sheets and evaluation forms to measure an instructor's competence, effectiveness, and instructional skills.

Cost analyses: Training managers calculate the cost of instructors' fees, materials, facilities, travel, training time, and the number of trainees to determine the hourly cost of training for each participant.

✓ Chapter 1 Knowledge Check

1. Which of the following is not a key benefit of the evaluation function?

    a. Improves the design of the learning experience

    b. Determines whether objectives were met and to what extent

    c. Determines the cause of the performance gap and appropriate remediation

    d. Assesses the effectiveness and appropriateness of instructional strategies

2. Which of the following most accurately describes performance agreement and the importance of objectives when conducting evaluation?

    a. Ensuring that every objective has a corresponding evaluation task

    b. Assessing the effectiveness of a training program while it's in development

    c. Assessing the effectiveness of a training program when it's completed and has been pilot-tested

    d. Assessing the impact of training transfer

3. Which of the following best describes formative evaluation?

    a. Ensuring that every objective has a corresponding evaluation task

    b. Assessing the effectiveness of a training program while it's in development

    c. Assessing the effectiveness of a training program when it's completed and has been pilot-tested

    d. Assessing the impact of training transfer

4. Which of the following best describes summative evaluation?

    a. Ensuring that every objective has a corresponding evaluation task

    b. Assessing the effectiveness of a training program while it's in development

    c. Assessing the effectiveness of a training program when it's completed and has been pilot-tested

    d. Assessing the impact of training transfer

5. Which of Kirkpatrick's four levels of evaluation assesses the learner's ability to transfer learning on the job and usually occurs three months to one year after the training event?

    a. Level 1

    b. Level 2

    c. Level 3

    d. Level 4

6. Which of Kirkpatrick's four levels of evaluation assesses the learner's reaction to the training program and is usually administered at the end of the training event?

   a. Level 1

   b. Level 2

   c. Level 3

   d. Level 4

7. Which of the following best describes a reliable instrument?

   a. The extent to which an instrument is consistent enough that subsequent measures of an item give the same approximate results

   b. The extent to which the instrument represents the content of the program

   c. The degree to which an instrument represents the construct it was meant to represent

   d. The extent to which an instrument agrees with the results of other instruments administered at approximately the same time to measure the same characteristics

8. Which of the following best describes construct validity?

   a. The extent to which an instrument is consistent enough that subsequent measures of an item give the same approximate results

   b. The extent to which the instrument represents the content of the program

   c. The degree to which an instrument represents the construct it was meant to represent

   d. The extent to which an instrument agrees with the results of other instruments administered at approximately the same time to measure the same characteristics

9. Which of the following best describes concurrent validity?

   a. The extent to which an instrument is consistent enough that subsequent measures of an item give the same approximate results

   b. The extent to which the instrument represents the content of the program

   c. The degree to which an instrument represents the construct it was meant to represent

   d. The extent to which an instrument agrees with the results of other instruments administered at approximately the same time to measure the same characteristics

10. Which evaluation model focuses on cost-benefit ratio and calculating ROI?

    a. Level 2

    b. Level 3

    c. Level 4

    d. Level 5

11. According to Tyler's goal attainment model, the objectives—the ends of instruction—are identified first.

    a. True

    b. False

12. According to the PBT model, learners must demonstrate knowledge or skills prior to leaving the class or instruction.

    a. True

    b. False

References

Barksdale, S., and T. Lund. (2001). *Rapid Evaluation.* Alexandria, VA: ASTD Press.

Basarab, D. and D. Root. (1992). *The Training Evaluation Process: A Practical Approach to Evaluating Corporate Training Programs.* New York: Springer.

Bloom, B., T. Hastings, and G.F. Madaus. (1971). *Handbook of Formative and Summative Evaluation of Student Learning.* New York: McGraw-Hill.

Conway, M., and M. Cassidy. (2001). "Evaluating Trainer Effectiveness." *Infoline* No. 250103.

Conway, M., and S. Thomas. (2003). "Using Electronic Surveys." *Infoline* No. 250301.

Herschbach, D.R. (Spring 1992). "Technology and Efficiency: Competencies as Content." *Journal of Technology Education* 3 (2), pp. 15-25.

Kaplan, R., and D. Norton. (1996). *The Balanced Scorecard.* Boston: Harvard Business Press.

Kirkpatrick, D. (1998). *Evaluating Training Programs: The Four Levels.* San Francisco, CA: Berrett-Koehler.

Long, L. (1998). "Surveys From Start to Finish." *Infoline* No. 258612.

Marshall, V., and R. Schriver. (January 1994). "Using Evaluation to Improve Performance." *Technical and Skills Training,* pp. 6-9.

McArdle, G.E. (1999). *Training Design and Delivery.* Alexandria, VA: ASTD Press.

McCain, D.V. (2005). *Evaluation Basics.* Alexandria, VA: ASTD Press.

Phillips, J. (1998). "Level 1 Evaluation: Reaction and Planned Action." *Infoline* No. 259813.

———. (1998). "Level 2 Evaluation: Learning." *Infoline* No. 259814.

Phillips, J., P.P. Phillips, and T. Hodges. (2004). *Make Training Evaluation Work.* Alexandria, VA: ASTD Press.

Phillips, J, P.P. Phillips, and W. Wurtz. (1998). "Level 5 Evaluation: Mastering ROI." *Infoline* No. 259805.

Salkind, N.J. (2005). *Tests & Measurement for People Who (Think They) Hate Tests and Measurement.* Thousand Oaks, CA: Sage Publications.

Sasser, E.W., L.A. Schlesinger, and J.L. Heskett. (1997). *The Service Profit Chain.* New York: Free Press.

Scriven, M. (1967). "The Methodology of Evaluation." In R.W. Tyler, et al., eds. *Perspectives in Evaluation, American Educational Research Association Monograph Series on Curriculum Evaluation.* No. 1. Chicago: Rand McNally.

Smith, D., and J. Blakesell. (September 2002). "The New Strategic Six Sigma." *T+D,* pp. 45-52.

Tanquist, S. (2000). "Evaluating E-Learning." *Infoline* No. 250009.

Tyler, R. (1949). *Basic Principles of Curriculum and Instruction.* Chicago: University of Chicago Press.

Waagen, A.K. (1997). "Essentials for Evaluation." *Infoline* No. 259705.

Wholey, J.S., H.P. Hatry, and K.E. Newcomer. (2004). *Handbook of Practical Program Evaluation.* 2nd edition. San Francisco: Jossey-Bass.

2
Statistical Theory and Methods

Statistics allow workplace learning and performance (WLP) professionals to quantitatively describe and draw inferences about people, things, or events. In other words, statistics allow data to be organized and summarized and make it possible to draw generalizations and inferences. Statistics enable WLP professionals to document current levels of performance (individual, group, or organizational), measure the impact of their programs, and offer well-grounded feedback for change.

For many WLP professionals, the use of statistics is an onerous task—but it shouldn't be. Several software applications can do the number crunching for trainers; however, practitioners must understand how to use statistics. The selection and interpretation of statistics still rests in their hands. To use statistics properly, a statistics consumer needs to understand some essential concepts and principles. Although this chapter is designed to serve as a primer for statistics, occasionally calculations are used to help understanding.

WLP professionals must have a broad understanding of how data falls into distributions (for example, variance and normal distribution) and how data relates to other data (for example, correlation and regression). In addition, from an inferential standpoint, WLP professionals must understand concepts related to hypothesis testing, such as effect sizes and confidence intervals. It's easy to misuse or misinterpret statistics. Having a real understanding of statistics means that people can apply them correctly, represent findings accurately, and draw appropriate inferences.

Learning Objectives:

- ☑ Define and illustrate the three measures of central tendency.
- ☑ Define and compare the various types of frequency distributions.
- ☑ Express how measurement scales and statistical implications are used in the collection of measurement data.
- ☑ Explain how the measures of variance are used in statistics.
- ☑ Describe how distributions are used with standard scores.
- ☑ Identify the correct usage of correlation versus causation in data.
- ☑ List the five steps in the hypothesis-testing process.
- ☑ Demonstrate knowledge related to effect sizes and confidence intervals.
- ☑ Recognize the appropriate use of statistical information.

Measures of Central Tendency (Averages)

Besides using descriptive statistics for charts and graphs, trainers can perform several numeric calculations on them. The most common are called *measures of central tendency*, or *averages,* of which there are three: *mean, median,* and *mode.* Each type of average serves a unique purpose.

Mean

The *mean score* is considered the most robust, or least affected by the presence of extreme values (outliers), of the three types of central tendency measures, because each number in the data set has an impact on its (mean) value.

The mean is represented by the following formula:

Mean = Sum of all numbers divided by the number of values that make up the sum

The mean is a good measure of central tendency for roughly symmetric distributions but can be misleading in skewed, or nonsymmetric, distributions because it can be influenced a great deal by extreme scores. Therefore, other statistics, such as the median, may be more informative and appropriate for distributions that are often quite skewed, such as reaction time or family income.

Median

The *median* is the middle of a distribution arranged by magnitude: Half the scores are above the median, and half are below the median. The median is less sensitive to extreme scores than the mean, which makes it a better measure than the mean for highly skewed distributions. The median income is usually more informative than the mean income, for example.

The median in a distribution of odd- or even-numbered values, as noted in Table 1-1, is the calculated average of the two numbers of the high and low side of the *n*th number in the formula.

Which of these two measures—the sample mean or median—should trainers use? It depends. Usually medians are a better measure for skewed distributions than means, but this guideline must be tempered by common sense. In a dispute between the American Medical Association and the American Bar Association about the rising costs of malpractice insurance for doctors, the doctors used means to show a sharp rise in costs in the period 1980 to 1984, and the lawyers used medians to show that there was no rise at all (Schwarz 1998).

Mode

The *mode,* the most frequently occurring score in a distribution, is also used as a measure of central tendency. The advantage of the mode as a measure of central tendency is that its meaning is obvious. Further, it's the only measure of central tendency that can be used with nominal data.

The mode is greatly subject to sample fluctuations, so it's not recommended for use as the only measure of central tendency. A further disadvantage of the mode is that many distributions have more than one mode; these distributions are called *multimodal.*

The mean score is considered the most robust of the three types of central tendency because each number in the data set has an impact on the value of the mean. The median and the mode can be unaffected by individual numbers.

Table 2-1 shows a sample set of data collected by a trainer. These scores represent the pretest scores on a knowledge test a trainer administered before the start of a training program. This data is used to show the three types of measures of central tendency as well as variance.

Table 2-1. Pretest Scores (Arranged From High to Low)

Scores (x)	Mode (mo)	Median (mdn)[a]
29	The mode is the most frequently occurring number	mdn=(n+1)÷2
35		
37		mdn=(12+1)÷2
37		
46	mo=37	mdn=6.5th number
52		
56		mdn=54
59		
61		
73		
77		
82		
$\sum x$=644		
The number of values, n, equals 12 The mean = $\sum x÷n$ The mean = 644 ÷12=53.67		

$\sum x$ = sum of values in the list
n = number of values in the list
a Note that the formula in the example applies only to a case with an even number of values. For the odd number of values it is not necessary to average the two middle values to come up with the "virtual median." In the case of an odd number, the appropriate formula is (n+1÷2) ÷2.

Frequency Distributions

A set of numbers may be summarized in two major ways: using pictures and using summary numbers. Each method has advantages and disadvantages, and the use of one method need not exclude the use of the other. This section describes drawing pictures of data called *frequency distributions.*

A frequency distribution can show the actual number of observations falling in each range or percentage of observations. With percentage of observations, the distribution is called a *relative frequency distribution.*

Some conditions that a frequency distribution might illustrate include dispersion, clusters, skewness, outliers, and normal distribution. The next section explores these concepts in more depth.

Definition of Terms

Confounding variable is an unknown or uncontrolled variable that produces an effect in an experimental setting. A confounding variable is an "independent variable" that the evaluator didn't somehow recognize or control. It becomes a variable that confounds the experiment.

Continuous variable is a variable whose quantification can be broken down into extremely small units (for example, time, speed, distance).

Control group is a group of participants in an experiment that's equal in all ways to the experimental group except that it didn't receive the experimental treatment.

Covariates are the multiple dependent variables in a study with multiple independent variables.

Dependent variable is frequently thought of as the "outcome," or treatment variable. The dependent variable's outcome depends on the independent variable and covariates.

Dichotomous variable is a variable that falls into one of two possible classifications (for example, gender [male or female]). An artificially dichotomous variable is imposed for classification purposes (for example, age classified as retired [>65] or not retired [<65]).

Discrete variable is a variable in which the units are in whole numbers, or "discrete" units (for example, number of children, number of defects).

Experimental group is the treatment group; those participants who receive the "treatment," for example, the training program.

Independent variable is the variable that influences the dependent variable. Age, seniority, gender, shift, level of education, and so on may all be factors (independent variables) that influence a person's performance (the dependent variable).

Definition of Terms, continued

Nominal data includes the numbers or variables used to classify a system, as in a telephone number or the numbers on a football player's jersey.

Ordinal data includes the numbers or variables that allow ranking the order of importance from highest to lowest.

Randomization is a method that helps diffuse the covariates across the experimental and control groups. Researchers in organizations often have multiple dependent variables to deal with but typically want to compare one dependent variable to one independent variable (for example, performance in a training program—an independent variable—to job performance—a dependent variable).

Standard deviation is a commonly used measure or indicator of the amount of variability of scores from the mean. The standard deviation is a statistic that's often used in formulas for advanced or inferential statistics.

Treatment (experimental) variable is the term researchers and statisticians use to define the "manipulated" variable in an experiment. An experimental group receives a treatment (for example, attends a training program), and a control group does not.

Measures of Dispersion

There are several measures of *dispersion*, the most common being the standard deviation. These measures indicate to what degree the observations of a data set are dispersed, or spread out, around their mean. In manufacturing or measurement, high precision is associated with low dispersion.

Skewness

Skewness is defined as asymmetry in the distribution of sample data values. Values on one side of the distribution tend to be farther from the middle than values on the other side.

For skewed data, the usual measures of location give different values; for example, mode < median < mean would indicate positive (or right) skewness. Positive (or right) skewness is more common than negative (or left) skewness.

Outliers

An *outlier* is a data point that's far removed in value from the others in the data set. It's an unusually large or unusually small value compared with the others. An outlier might be the result of an error in measurement, in which case it distorts interpretation of the data, having undue influence on many summary statistics (for example, the mean).

If an outlier is a genuine result, it's important because it might indicate an extreme of behavior in the process under study. For this reason, all outliers must be examined carefully before embarking on any formal analysis. Outliers should not be routinely removed without further justification.

Normal Distribution

The term ***normal distribution*** refers to a particular way in which observations tend to pile up around a certain value instead of being spread evenly across a range of values. The normal distribution is generally most applicable to continuous data, and it's intrinsically associated with parametric statistics, which are methods to test statistical hypotheses that assume the distribution of variables falls into known families of probability distributions. Graphically, the normal distribution is best described by a ***bell-shaped curve.*** This curve is described in terms of the point at which its height is maximum—its mean—and how wide it is—its standard deviation.

Measurement Scales, Variables, and Classifications

WLP professionals are constantly collecting data, whether they know it or not. Evaluation sheets from training programs, questionnaires and surveys, training program cost data, program development costs, and needs analysis results all represent data. Being able to understand and interpret data is what discriminates a novice from a seasoned professional.

An important, yet often overlooked, concept pertains to classification of data. Knowing what type of data a trainer has is a prerequisite to knowing what kinds of manipulations can be performed on data. Trainers must understand levels of data and be aware of each piece of data they work with. For example, even a short two-page questionnaire may have up to 100 codable data points, each with its own level of data. There are four primary classifications of data: nominal, ordinal, interval, and ratio.

Nominal Data

Nominal data, the lowest type of data, provides a classification of categories. From a statistical perspective, this type of data permits codifying the classification of items or things that vary into groups. The numbers on a football team's jerseys are an example of nominal data, as are digits of a telephone number. The purpose of nominal data is merely to classify or identify units within a larger system. It makes no sense to perform an arithmetic operation (addition, subtraction, multiplication, division) on this type of data.

The mean has no value for nominal data, but the mode, as a measure of central tendency, is appropriate for use with nominal data. Nominal scales can also be used to label topics of interest or categories, as in this example:

Which fringe benefit is most important to you?

1. Health insurance

2. Disability insurance

3. 401(k)

The correct and only statistic trainers can use in measuring the outcome of responses to this nominally scaled question is the mode—that is, the answer selected most frequently.

Ordinal Data

Ordinal data makes it possible to rank order items measured in terms of which has less and which has more of the quality represented by the variable, but this type of data doesn't tell how much more or less. Ordinal data has all the characteristics of nominal data but also conveys a rank order of importance, from lowest to highest. Here's an example:

How many hours per week do you prefer to work?

1. 40 to 42 hours

2. 43 to 45 hours

3. 46 to 48 hours

4. 49 or more hours

In addition to calculating the mode, ordinals allow calculating the median—the category in which the 50th percentile falls. In addition, percentiles other than the 50th, such as the 25th or 75th, can be determined.

Interval Data

Interval data allows not only rank ordering the items measured, but also quantifying and comparing the sizes of differences between them. For example, temperature, as measured in degrees Fahrenheit or Celsius, constitutes an interval scale. It can be said that a temperature of 40 degrees is higher than a temperature of 30 degrees and that an increase from 20 to 40 degrees is twice as much as an increase from 30 to 40 degrees.

Interval responses are even more powerful than ordinal and nominal scales because the differences between scale values can be interpreted meaningfully. Here's an example, with the numbers one through six being values:

How likely are you to take additional college coursework?

1. Will definitely not

2. Extremely unlikely

3. Unlikely

4. Likely

5. Extremely likely

6. Will definitely

Although respondents are ranking their likelihood of taking additional coursework (ordinal), the scale is such that there's statistical difference in the value (interval), and this value is the same between each choice. Often this value is assumed to exist, when in reality, the numbers are used for coding purposes rather than evidence of statistical meaning. With these responses, trainers can calculate the mode, median, and mean. Because the mean can be calculated, the standard deviation—that is, the degree of deviation from the mean—can also be calculated. Also, in an interval-level seven-point scale, for example, the difference between a rating of 2 and 4 (2) has the same degree of difference as between a rating of 5 and 7 (also 2).

Ratio Data

Ratio data is similar to interval data; in addition to all the properties of interval variables, ratio variables feature an identifiable absolute zero point, which means they allow for statements such as "x is two times more than y." Typical examples of ratio scales are measures of time and measures of space. For example, the Kelvin temperature scale is a ratio scale, so it can be stated that not only is a temperature of 200 degrees higher than one of 100 degrees, but also that it's twice as high. Interval scales do not have the ratio property. Most statistical data analysis procedures don't distinguish between the interval and ratio properties of measurement scales.

Therefore, the ratio scale is the most analytically versatile because the responses have an unambiguous starting point, zero, unlike the other scales. Here's an example:

What were the total salaries paid in your division last year?

If the response is $110,000 one year and $99,000 the next, it can be stated that salaries were reduced by 10 percent.

Furthermore, ratio scale responses carry the same statistical power as interval scale responses.

Measures of Dispersion (Variation)

Variation, also known as *dispersion,* is another of the most practical statistical concepts; it's useful for summarizing large amounts of information. The variance is a measure of how spread out a distribution is. Variance combines all the values in a data set to produce a measure of spread. Variance (symbolized by S^2) and standard deviation (the square root of the variance, symbolized by S) are the most commonly used measures of spread.

Variance is calculated as the average squared deviation of each number from the mean of its data set:

Variance (S^2) = Squared deviation from the mean ÷ Number of observations

For example, for the numbers 1, 2, and 3, the mean is 2 and the variance is 0.667, as shown in this calculation:

Variance$=[(1-2)^2+(2-2)^2+(3-2)^2]\div3=0.667$

Calculating variance involves squaring deviations, so it doesn't have the same unit of measurement as the original observations. For example, lengths measured in meters (m) have a variance measured in meters squared (m^2). Taking the square root of the variance gives the units used in the original scale, and this is the standard deviation.

Standard Deviation

Standard deviation is the measure of spread most commonly used in statistical practice when the mean is used to calculate central tendency. Therefore, it measures spread around the mean:

Standard deviation (S) = Square root of the variance

Because of its close links with the mean, standard deviation can be greatly affected if the mean gives a poor measure of central tendency.

Standard deviation can be interpreted graphically. Many data sets have a distribution similar to that shown in Figure 2-1. For these data sets, the standard deviation is the distance on either side of the mean (average) to include 68 percent of the population. If twice this distance (two standard deviations) were considered, it could be expected to include 95 percent of the population. If three times the distance (three standard deviations) were considered, it would be expected to include 99 percent of the population.

Standard deviation is also influenced by outliers; one value could contribute largely to the results of the standard deviation. In that sense, the standard deviation is a good indicator of the presence of outliers. This makes standard deviation a useful measure of spread for symmetrical distributions with no outliers.

Standard deviation is also useful in comparing the spreads of two separate data sets that have approximately the same means. The data set with the smaller standard deviation has a narrower spread of measurements around the mean and, therefore, usually has comparatively fewer high or low values. A question selected at random from a data set with a low standard deviation has a better chance of being close to the mean than an item from a data set with a higher standard deviation.

Generally, the more widely spread the values, the larger the standard deviation. For example, imagine separating two different sets of exam results from a class of 30 students; the first exam has marks ranging from 31 percent to 98 percent, and the other ranges from 82 percent to 93 percent. Given these ranges, the standard deviation would be larger for the results of the first exam.

Figure 2-1. Sample Deviation and the Bell Curve

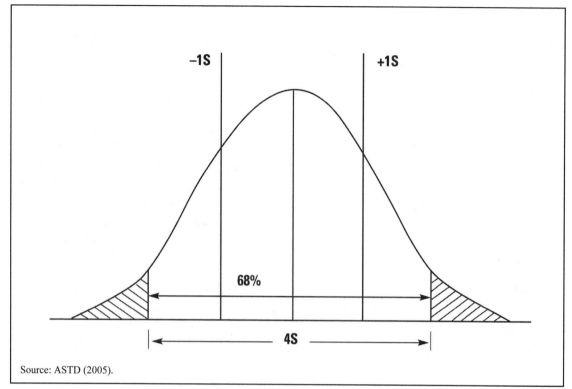

Source: ASTD (2005).

When using standard deviation, keep in mind the following properties:

- Standard deviation is used only to measure spread or dispersion around the mean of a data set.

- Standard deviation is never negative.

- Standard deviation is sensitive to outliers. A single outlier can raise the standard deviation and, in turn, distort the picture of spread.

- For data with approximately the same mean, the greater the spread, the greater the standard deviation.

- If all values of a data set are the same, the standard deviation is zero (because each value is equal to the mean).

Distributions and Standard Scores

Standard scores allow raw scores on any test to be compared, and they make interpretation of test scores clearer. Raw test scores—that is, the number correct—are converted to reflect equally where they fall with respect to the mean. Therefore, standard scores are ***transformed scores.*** They provide a way to standardize or equate different metrics to allow making comparisons. They can be used to determine where a person's score falls in comparison with another person or in comparison with the group. For example, percentiles, a common form of standard scores, may be used to indicate how a person's score compares with others on a scale of one to 100. They are especially important when using tests that have been standardized on large populations reflecting the demographic characteristics of the population as a whole.

Most educational and psychological tests use standard scores to report test results. Standard scores are based on the bell-shaped, normal curve. It's important to understand the mean and the standard deviation to understand how these standard test scores are used. The bell-shaped curve shows that test scores can easily be compared by using the standard score model.

Correlation

The key purpose of **correlation** is to measure the relationship between two or more variables—but correlation should not be used to prove causation. Correlation shows a prediction for Y given X. For example, college admissions officers often use high school grade averages to predict college averages. So if a student has a 3.2 GPA in high school, it can be predicted that he or she would earn close to a 3.2 in college, given that admissions officers have determined a close to perfect positive correlation between high school and college grade point averages.

To test for a cause-and-effect connection between variables, researchers must have a highly controlled experiment environment. As the degree of control is lost, or when researchers try to work with existing data, they may have to settle for a relational study. In a relational study, relationships, but not cause-and-effect connections, can be inferred.

Relational studies use a statistic called a **correlation coefficient.** A correlation coefficient is always expressed as a number between −1.00 and +1.00 that describes the strength and direction of the relationship between two variables. A correlation coefficient value of +1.00 represents a perfect positive relationship between two variables, X and Y; each value of X is the same value for Y. If each pair of X and Y values are plotted on a scatter plot (a chart with X and Y axes), the values fall along a straight line, starting at the lower left and increasing upward along a 45-degree line. For example, there's a positive relationship (strong but typical—not perfect) between increases in outside air temperatures in the summer and ice cream sales.

A −1.00 indicates a perfect negative relationship: If one variable is high, the other is low. In other words, a negative relationship shows an inverse relationship between the two variables. For example, there's an inverse, or negative, relationship between energy consumption for heating homes and outdoor temperature: As temperatures drop, energy consumption increases. The complete absence of a relationship is indicated by a coefficient of 0.00. In this case, it's impossible to use an X value to predict a Y value.

For a set of variable pairs, the correlation coefficient gives the strength of the association. The line that can be fitted to the plot of X and Y value pairs showing the relation between variables is called the **regression line,** which is defined as the best-fitting straight line through all value pairs.

Statistical Inference and Hypothesis Testing

The purpose of inferential statistics is to test a (null) hypothesis and then accept or fail to accept (reject) the hypothesis. Generally speaking, practitioners should always test a null hypothesis—stating that they expect no difference between the treatment group (the "before" group) and the control group (the "after" group).

The hypothesis-testing process consists of five steps:

1. *State the hypothesis.* For example, there's no significant difference in worker attitude toward participating in quality circles before and after a two-hour quality circle orientation program.

2. *Select a significance level.* The significance level defines for researchers how rigorously they will remain with the null hypothesis before not accepting it. The significance level is always stated as a probability level—that is, how confident researchers are that their results occurred because of the effect of the treatment and not by chance. The $p=0.05$ level (five times out of 100) and the $p=0.01$ (one time out of 100) measures are the most frequently used significance levels. The $p=0.01$ level is the more rigorous of the two.

3. *Compute or calculate the statistic.* In this step, the researcher calculates the statistic based on the formula for the selected statistic.

4. *Obtain the critical value.* The critical value is the criterion measure or the cutoff point for the significance level (step 2) that has been selected.

5. *Accept or reject the null hypothesis.* The final step requires researchers to accept or reject the null hypothesis. If the critical value exceeds the calculated value, the researcher accepts the null hypothesis. If the critical value is less than the calculated value, the researcher rejects the null hypothesis.

In English, *significant* means important, whereas in statistics, it means probably true (not caused by chance). A research finding may be true without being important. When statisticians say a result is "highly significant," they mean it's very probably true. They do not (necessarily) mean it's highly important.

In the past, researchers merely had go or no-go decisions about whether their calculated value exceeded the critical value, never really knowing the exact significance level obtained. Now, instead of accepting or rejecting a hypothesis at a predetermined significance level, researchers actually know the *exact* probability of an event occurring by chance. The $p=0.05$ and $p=0.01$ levels of significance remain benchmarks for the rigor of scientific investigation. Instead of having to use the tedious five-step process previously described, practitioners can use computer-based statistical software.

Most significance tests assume that users have a truly random sample. If a sample isn't truly random, a significance test may overstate the accuracy of results because it considers only random error. The test can't consider biases resulting from nonrandom error (for example, a badly selected sample).

These are some key concepts about statistical significance:

- In statistical terms, *significant* does not necessarily mean important.
- Probability values should be read in reverse.
- Too many significance tests turn up some falsely significant relationships.
- It's important to check the sampling procedure to avoid bias.

Effect Sizes

Effect size is a way of quantifying the difference between two groups. For example, if one group (the treatment group) has had an experimental treatment and the other (the control group) has not, the effect size is a measure of the effectiveness between the two groups. Effect size uses standard deviation to contextualize the difference between the two groups.

Confidence Intervals

The *confidence interval* is the range where something is expected to be. Saying "expected" leaves open the possibility of being wrong. The degree of confidence measures the probability of that expectation to be true.

The degree of confidence is linked with the width of the confidence interval. It's easy to be very confident that something will be within a very wide range, and vice versa. Also, the amount of information (typically related to the sample size) has an influence on the degree of confidence and the width of the confidence interval. With more information, there can be more confidence that what's being measured will be within a given interval. Also, with more information and keeping a given degree of confidence, the interval can be narrowed.

For example, say a survey is conducted in Alexandria, Virginia. The question is "Do you prefer Coca-Cola or Pepsi?" Of the responses, 60 percent answer Coca-Cola, and 40 percent answer Pepsi. So the estimation is that, in this city, 60 percent prefer Coca-Cola. This doesn't mean that 60 percent of the population in this city prefers Coca-Cola—unless everyone in the population answered the survey. However, there's some "confidence" that the actual proportion of people choosing Coca-Cola will be within some interval around the 60 percent found in the sample. The amount of confidence depends on how wide the interval is. If the survey is based on a sample of 100 people, there can be 90 percent confidence that the actual proportion of those preferring Coca-Cola will be between 52 percent and 68 percent. Also, there can be 99 percent confidence that the actual proportion will be between 48 percent and 72 percent (for the same sample size, with more confidence and a wider interval). If the survey had been on a sample of 1,000 people instead of 100, there could be 90 percent confidence that the actual proportion is between 57.5 percent and 62.5 percent (compared with 52 percent and 68 percent for the same confidence with a sample of 100). Keep in mind that the larger the sample, the higher the degree of confidence.

Appropriate Use of Statistical Information and Data

As Mark Twain said, "Collecting data is like collecting garbage. Pretty soon, we have to do something with it." If not used properly, statistical information and evaluation data are useless. Improper use of evaluation data can lead to four major problems:

- Too many organizations don't use evaluation data at all. In these situations, data is collected, tabulated, catalogued, filed, and never used by any particular group other than the person who initially collected the data.

- Data is not provided to the appropriate groups. Different groups need different types of data and often in very different formats. Analyzing target audiences and determining the specific data needed for each group are important for communicating data.

- Data isn't used to drive improvement. Most evaluation data uncovers process improvement opportunities and identifies features that could be adjusted or changes that should be made to make the program more effective. If it's not part of the feedback cycle, evaluation falls short of what it's intended to do.

- Data is used for the wrong reasons—to take action against a person or a group or to withhold funds rather than improve processes. Sometimes the data is used in political ways to gain power or advantage over another person.

These problems represent dysfunctional activities that can destroy evaluation processes. They must be addressed if evaluation is to add value.

✓ Chapter 2 Knowledge Check

1. Which of the following best describes a situation where the mode < median < mean?

    a. Negative skewness

    b. Positive skewness

    c. Outlier

    d. Normal distribution

2. Which of the following best describes normal distribution?

    a. An observation in a data set that's far removed in value from others in the data set

    b. The symmetry in the distribution of the same data values

    c. The way in which observations tend to pile up around the mean, also known as the bell-shaped curve

    d. Variation in values that could be widely scattered or tightly clustered

3. Which of the following best describes dispersion?

    a. An observation in a data set that's far removed in value from the others in the data set

    b. The symmetry in the distribution of the same data values

    c. The way in which observations tend to pile up around the mean, also known as the bell-shaped curve

    d. Variation in values that could be widely scattered or tightly clustered

4. Which of the following best describes an outlier?

    a. An observation in a data set that's far removed in value from the others in the data set

    b. The symmetry in the distribution of the same data values

    c. The way in which observations tend to pile up around the mean, also known as the bell-shaped curve

    d. Variation in values that could be widely scattered or tightly clustered

5. Which of the following types of data make it possible to rank order items measured in terms of which has less or more of the quality represented?

    a. Nominal

    b. Ordinal

    c. Interval

    d. Ratio

6. Which of the following types of data include the feature of identifying an absolute zero point?

   a. Nominal

   b. Ordinal

   c. Interval

   d. Ratio

7. Variance is defined as how spread out a distribution of data points is, whereas the standard deviation is the measure of how spread out the data points are when the mean is used to calculate central tendency.

   a. True

   b. False

8. The reason that practitioners convert raw scores to standard scores includes which of the following?

   a. To indicate the number of correct answers to allow scores to be compared

   b. To reflect where they fall with respect to the mean to allow scores to be compared and interpreted

   c. To understand the cause-and-effect connections between variables

   d. Because they are always expressed as a number between −1.00 and +1.00

9. An example of a relational study statistic that measures the relationship between two or more variables includes

   a. Correlation coefficient

   b. Cause-and-effect connection

   c. Normal distribution

   d. Skewness

10. The primary goal of hypothesis testing is to test a hypothesis and then accept or reject the hypothesis based on the findings.

    a. True

    b. False

References

Bluman, A.G. (2003). *Elementary Statistics: A Step by Step Approach.* 2nd edition. New York: McGraw-Hill.

Grant, E.L., and R.S. Leavenworth. (1996). *Statistical Quality Control.* 7th edition. New York: McGraw-Hill

Kearsley, G. (1982). *Cost, Benefits, & Productivity in Training Systems.* Boston: Addison-Wesley.

Martelli, J.T., and D. Mathern. (1991). "Statistics for HRD Practice." *Infoline* No. 259101.

Phillips, J.J., P.P. Phillips, and T. Hodges. (2004). *Make Training Evaluation Work.* Alexandria, VA: ASTD Press.

Popham, W.J. (1973). *Educational Statistics: Use and Interpretation.* New York: Harper and Row.

Rumsey, D. (2003). *Statistics for Dummies.* Indianapolis, IN: Wiley Publishing.

Schwartz, C.J. (1998). "Mean, Median, and Mode." Available at: http://www.math.sfu.ca/~cschwarz/Stat-301/Handouts/node30.html.

3
Research Design

WLP professionals need to know how to design research methods to be able to implement measurement and evaluation activities, assess proposed methods, and make recommendations on how to implement a measurement and evaluation activity. Expertise in this area benefits a WLP professional by providing the foundation for implementing measurement and evaluation activities and is part of the instructional design phase of analysis and evaluation. This knowledge area outlines the knowledge required to design research, including items to consider when selecting tools, defining populations, and collecting data. This knowledge area gives WLP professionals enough detail to get started designing a research activity as well as supplemental references and resources to use when designing a research activity.

Learning Objectives:

- ☑ List and discuss the major concepts and issues related to research design.
- ☑ Identify the main sources of measurement error, including the various forms of bias.
- ☑ Describe the basic rights of human subjects (participants).
- ☑ Name and describe three tools for identifying problems within an organization.
- ☑ Outline the steps in research design development.
- ☑ List and discuss the advantages and disadvantages of various data collection methods.
- ☑ Describe one data organization methodology and its components.
- ☑ List several types of data storage.
- ☑ Discuss data management and security.

Concepts and Issues

Research design for measuring and evaluating training and development is critical to the success of the evaluation. The following sections describe several major concepts related to research design.

Dependent, Independent, and Extraneous Variables

The concept of independent and dependent variables is used in introductory algebra. For example, in the equation $F=1.8*C+32$ used to convert the current temperature from Fahrenheit to Celsius, C (Celsius) is the independent variable, and F (Fahrenheit) is the dependent variable. If the equation were written as $C=(F-32)\div1.8$, C would be the dependent variable and F the independent variable.

In the temperature conversion example, it doesn't matter which way the equation is written. When running an experiment, however, it's best for the independent variable to correspond to factors that are being varied and the dependent variable be the one that's measured.

The independent variable is controlled by the evaluator, who splits participants into different groups, with each group associated with a different treatment (or value) of the independent variable. The treatment can simply be to identify what group a participant falls in, or it can be associated with a numeric value. The independent variable is the influencing variable; dependent variables are the influenced variables.

One example involves comparing how fast subjects complete a web-browsing task when using the Netscape and Internet Explorer browsers. In this case, the independent variable would be "web browser," and the treatments of that variable would be "Netscape" and "Internet Explorer." This variable simply classifies the web browser, so it's measured on a nominal scale. The completion of the task is the dependent variable.

An example of treatments being numeric might occur if performance is being measured as the area of a onscreen window that varies. In that case, the independent variable would be "window area," and the treatments might be 100, 150, and 200 square inches. In both examples, participants are divided into a fixed number of treatment groups for the independent variable(s), but in the second case, it might (or might not) be possible to develop a mathematical equation relating window area to task performance.

Extraneous variables are undesirable variables that influence the relationship between the variables an evaluator is examining. Another way to think of them is that these variables influence an experiment's outcome, although they aren't actually the variables of interest. These variables are undesirable because they add error to an experiment. A major goal in research design is to decrease or control the influence of extraneous variables as much as possible.

Models and Measures

One of the biggest challenges when embarking on an organizational evaluation strategy is determining what results to measure and how to measure them. A measure is a standard used to assess the results of a performance intervention. It's essential to the evaluation to select measures before designing and developing the program.

The most important step in establishing measures for an evaluation is to validate the business drivers (Barksdale and Lund 2001). Business drivers are the internal and external forces that direct an organization's strategy, goals, business needs, and performance needs. External business drivers can include economics, human resources, government, public perception, and market or customer drivers. Internal business drivers are generated by internal decisions and can include technology; a change in system, process, or key policy; shareholder or financial drivers; and new product generation.

After identifying the business drivers and performance needs, the measurement approach can be determined. This measurement approach is centered most often on the level of Kirkpatrick's evaluation model to be used, but other models may be used as well. It's feasible to have three to five measures and corresponding approaches for the evaluation strategy, and then have different approaches for specific interventions. When considering specific evaluation approaches, a key discussion point should be determining how the specific solution approach rolls into the evaluation strategy measures.

The specific data for the solution should fit under the evaluation strategy umbrella. If a solution has a completely different parameter that doesn't fit, it's important to ask why and to determine whether the evaluation strategy may be missing an important factor or whether something else has changed in the environment and strategy maintenance is called for.

Research Questions

Research questions can be designed by using one or more of these formats:

- *Multiple choice questions* are used when all responses to questions can be included, when exclusivity can be constructed, and when bias resulting from the forced selection is insignificant.

- *Multiple answer questions* do not have exclusive answers; they are used to help respondents remember and to ensure that they consider all viable options.

- *Ranking questions* ask respondents to indicate, in order, their personal preferences and reveal the relative importance of the answers.

- *Open-ended questions* allow respondents to answer in their own words without prompting. Questions usually begin with who, what, when, where, why, or how.

- *Scaled questions* are used to determine opinions or attitudes by measuring direction (negative to positive) and intensity (strongly negative to strongly positive).

Wording in questionnaires is crucial because the success of a questionnaire depends on words alone. Questions that are open for interpretation could invalidate months of hard work.

When formulating questions, evaluators should define or qualify terms that could easily be misunderstood or misinterpreted, use gender-neutral wording, and define all acronyms. For questions with scales, such as agreement questions, the scale points should be placed in negative-to-positive order, for example, "strongly disagree" through "strongly agree." Including between five and nine response scale categories ensures that respondents will remember all the items. The WLP professional should avoid using leading questions, technical terminology, and questions that assume knowledge or experience respondents might not have.

Experimental Design

Measurement and evaluation are concerned with the analysis of data generated from an experiment. Practitioners should take time and effort to organize an experiment properly to ensure that the right type of data, and enough of it, is available to answer the questions of interest as clearly and efficiently as possible. This process is called *experimental design.*

Practitioners should clearly identify the specific questions that an experiment is intended to answer before carrying out the experiment. They should also attempt to identify known or expected sources of variability in experimental units because one of the main goals of a designed experiment is to reduce the effect of these sources of variability on answers to questions of interest. In other words, experiments should be designed to improve the precision of the answers.

Statistical and Design Control of Variables

A *control group* is a group of participants in an experiment that's equal in all ways to the experimental group, except the control group hasn't received the experimental treatment. A factor of an experiment is a controlled independent variable, a variable with levels set by the evaluator.

A factor is a general type or category of treatments. Different treatments constitute different levels of a factor. For example, say there are two groups of day shift employees, and one group receives training on telephone skills and one does not. Results are verified by customer satisfaction and other department metrics (such as call length). The workers are the experimental units, the training methods are the treatments, and the type of training method constitutes the level of the factor "type of training."

There are several experimental design models; these are some of the most common:

- *One-way analysis of variance:* This model allows comparing several groups of observations, all of which are independent but possibly with a different mean for each group. A test of great importance is whether all the means are equal. All observations arise from one of several different groups (or have been exposed to one of several different treatments in an experiment). This method classifies data one way, according to the group or treatment.

- *Two-way analysis of variance:* This model studies the effects of two factors separately (their main effects) and together (their interaction effect).

- *Completely randomized design:* This model assumes that treatments are allocated to experimental units completely at random.

- *Completely randomized block design:* In this design, participants are matched according to a variable that the evaluator wants to control. Participants are put into groups—known as *blocks*—of the same size as the number of treatments. The members of each block are then randomly assigned to different treatment groups.

Qualitative Research

Data collection methods are qualitative or quantitative. Quantitative methods result in what's called *hard data.* Hard data is objective and measurable, whether stated in terms of frequency, percentage, proportion, or time. Qualitative measures yield *soft data.* These types of measures are more intangible, anecdotal, personal, and subjective, as in opinions, attitudes, assumptions, feelings, values, and desires. Qualitative data can't be objectified, and that characteristic makes this type of data valuable. For example, knowing how job performers feel (qualitative measure) about a skill is just as important in a training program's final design as knowing how well (quantitative measure) they perform the skill.

Quantitative and qualitative measures can be combined in a data collection process for excellent results. For example, a qualitative method (say, interviews) can be used to collect anecdotes and examples. Then a quantitative method (such as a survey) can be developed, using the collected anecdotes and examples as survey items, to measure how many respondents fit the examples and how frequently the examples fit the respondents. Conversely, a quantitative method can be used first to collect information on frequency and number of respondents. Then a qualitative method can be used to flesh out survey items with richer detail. Qualitative and quantitative measures may also be combined in the same measurement tool. For example, items on a survey can be qualitative terms, such as feelings and opinions. How many times each item is chosen (frequency) is a quantitative measure.

Sampling

In simple terms, a *sample* is a portion of the population that an evaluator is interested in collecting data on. A sample should be a cross-section of the population, with all the characteristics of the population represented. For instance, with a corporate culture survey, every employee of the company is a member of the survey population, but if the company is large, the evaluator may be able to survey only a sample. To ensure that all characteristics of the population are represented in the sample, an evaluator needs to include some employees at every level. In a training evaluation survey, the population generally consists of learners and the people directly affected by learners' work, such as supervisors and subordinates. Representatives from all these groups must be included in the sample. To survey a cross-section of the population, the evaluator may have to use different versions or different types of surveys with different groups of people in the sample. For example, a survey devised to question support personnel about corporate culture may not be appropriate for managers. In addition, the sample must be large enough to be reliable—that is, the odds of having a question answered a certain way must be statistically equal.

To ensure that the sample meets these criteria, an evaluator should investigate the population to determine how large it is and the primary and secondary traits of its members. A *primary trait* is one the whole population has in common. A *secondary trait* is one that some, but not all, members of the population have in common.

An evaluator should choose a sampling method that allows for any primary and secondary traits the population displays. The two most common sampling methods are

- *Random sampling:* Each person in the population has a known and equal chance of being chosen for the sample. Choosing every tenth person from an alphabetical list of names, for example, creates a systematic random sample.

- *Stratified random sampling:* The population is divided into constituent parts, and then sample members are chosen randomly from the constituent parts. This method produces a more representative sample than the random sample because it take important differences in the population into account. For example, dividing the population into age groups (10–20, 21–30, 31–40, and so forth) and then randomly choosing people from each age group so that the proportion in the sample mirrors the same proportion in the population creates a stratified random sample.

Random Selection and Assignment

Random selection is the process of drawing the sample of people for a study from a population. *Random assignment* is the process of assigning the sample that's drawn to different groups or treatments in the study.

It's possible to have both random selection and random assignment in a study. Say that a random sample of 100 clients was drawn from a population list of 1,000 current clients of an organization. That's random sampling. Now say that 50 of these clients are randomly assigned to get some new additional treatment, and the other 50 are to be controls. That's random assignment.

It's also possible to have only one process (random selection or random assignment) but not the other in a study. For instance, if the 100 cases aren't randomly drawn from the list of 1,000 but instead are just the first 100 on the list, it's not random selection. However, an evaluator could still randomly assign this nonrandom sample to treatment versus control groups, or randomly select 100 from the list of 1,000 and then nonrandomly (haphazardly) assign them to treatment or control groups.

It's also possible to have neither random selection nor random assignment. In a typical nonequivalent group design in education, an evaluator might nonrandomly choose two fifth-grade classes to be in the study. This process is nonrandom selection. Then the evaluator could arbitrarily assign one class to get the new educational program and the other to be the control. This process is nonrandom (or nonequivalent) assignment.

Selection Bias

Selection bias is the error of distorting a statistical analysis by pre- or postselecting the samples. Typically, this process causes measures of statistical significance to appear much stronger than they are, but causing completely illusory artifacts is also possible. Selection bias can be the result of scientific fraud, which manipulates data directly, but more often it's unconscious or caused by biases in instruments used for observation. For example, astronomical observations typically find more blue galaxies than red ones simply because most instruments are more sensitive to blue light than to red light.

Sample Size Estimation

The size of the sample needed depends on

- the size of the population

- desired accuracy of results (that is, how much error is acceptable)

- the level of confidence that the results were not caused by chance.

Findings from samples are actually estimates for the overall population and, therefore, have some degree of inaccuracy or error. For example, the political and news polls on television and in newspapers typically give an error rate, such as ±3.5 percent, to indicate how accurate the figures are in relation to the overall population. This error rate indicates that the actual figure for the overall population is within ±3.5 percent of the estimate given. In general, the larger the sample size is in relation to the population size, the more accurate the estimate.

When using a sample, there's also a probability that the findings are caused merely by the random sample selected instead of being a true reflection of the population. Trainers need to decide how confident they want to be that the findings are real and not caused by chance. Typically, having one time in 20 that the findings were caused by chance is acceptable. This is called a 95 percent confidence interval, meaning that 19 times of 20, or 95 percent of the time, there is confidence that the findings are real, that is, the true population value the trainer is trying to estimate from the sample lies within the estimated value plus or minus the error. In some cases, an evaluator may decide that it's acceptable to have one time in 10 that the findings were caused by chance (that is, a 90 percent confidence interval).

If the size of the population is known, an acceptable error rate has been decided, and a level of confidence with results has been established, an evaluator can determine how large a sample is needed to meet those criteria. Figure 3-1 shows the sample size needed (in terms of percentage of population) to have an error rate of ±3.5 percent, with both a 95 percent confidence interval and a 90 percent confidence interval.

Figure 3-1. Determining Sample Size

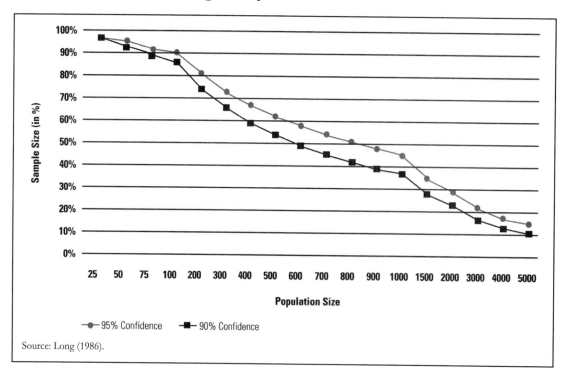

Source: Long (1986).

For example, if the population size is 200 and an evaluator wants to be 95 percent confident of the results, he or she should aim to get 80 percent of the population, or 160 people, to complete the survey. If the population size is 1,500, the evaluator needs to target only 34 percent of the total population.

Power Analysis

Performing power analysis and sample size estimation is an important aspect of experimental design because without these calculations, sample size may be too high or too low. If sample size is too low, the experiment will lack the precision to provide reliable answers to the questions it's investigating. If the sample size is too large, time and resources will be wasted, often for minimal gain.

In some power analysis software programs, a number of graphical and analytical tools are available to enable precise evaluation of the factors affecting power and sample size in many of the most commonly encountered statistical analyses. This information can be crucial to the design of a study that's cost effective and scientifically useful.

Properly designed experiments must ensure that power will be reasonably high to detect reasonable departures from the null hypothesis. Otherwise, an experiment is hardly worth doing. A number of factors influence power in a statistical test, including

- *The kind of statistical test being performed:* Some statistical tests are inherently more powerful than others.

- *Sample size:* In general, the larger the sample size, the larger the power. However, increasing sample size generally involves tangible costs in time, money, and effort. Consequently, it's important to make the sample size large enough but not wastefully large.

- *The size of experimental effects:* If the null hypothesis is wrong by a substantial amount, power will be higher than if it's wrong by a small amount.

- *The level of error in experimental measurements:* Measurement error acts as "noise" that can bury the "signal" of real experimental effects. Consequently, anything that enhances the accuracy and consistency of measurement can increase statistical power.

Sources of Measurement Error

The original development of research methods and instruments is subject to several types of bias. Sources of bias cut across all levels of evaluation.

Although addressing bias is difficult, it's not impossible. First, an evaluator should recognize that bias exists and then take action to minimize it. An evaluator can take steps to discern the types of bias that might be present and acknowledge them in communications. That way, credibility can be built by taking an appropriate, conservative approach when presenting results of the evaluation. Biased information or the failure to acknowledge sources of bias can taint results and calls into question the credibility of the evaluation effort.

Sampling Bias

The first type of bias is sampling bias. It's easy to send surveys or interviews to certain participants who are known and liked and are favorably disposed to the program. There's also a tendency to send information to recent participants who are usually still enthusiastic about the course and the opportunity to implement their action plans. The realities of the environment haven't dampened their spirits.

These practices can result in tainted data by introducing sampling bias. An evaluator should always conduct surveys or interviews with participants selected on a random basis.

Insufficient Sample Size

The second bias comes from not having a large enough sample. If a sample is drawn from the entire population—for example, all participants taking a course—the trainer may randomly select participants from each delivery of the course.

Observation Bias

The observation technique is not without bias problems. The more visible the observation process, the less reliable the data is. An observer who is not trained or provided with proper instruments adds to the data's unreliability. Therefore, observations should be conducted in the least obtrusive manner possible while still getting the needed information. Multiple observers are recommended. Training should be provided for observers as should some sort of a checklist, to aid in the observation.

Bias in Interviews and Focus Groups

Interviews and focus groups can provide high-quality information. To be most useful and to avoid bias, the interview design must ensure that

- the sample is representative of the population

- participants understand the questions

- participants are willing (their participation is not mandatory)

- the interviewer is trained in interviewing techniques and knows how to record the information accurately

- a protocol for consistency in questioning is in place

- a method to evaluate interview results objectively is used.

Central Tendency Bias

Some people hesitate to commit to either end of a scale and just indicate responses near the middle. This behavior is called the central tendency bias. For example, in a rating scale of 1 to 5, some raters tend to use the middle value, 3. An evaluator can address this source of bias by developing a scale with no middle value (such as 1 to 4) but must be sure to gather evidence that a scale with a middle position isn't working before dropping the middle value. This conclusion is best determined through a pilot test of the survey.

Facilitator Bias

Another source of bias may be facilitator or administrator bias toward test participants or the subject being evaluated. For example, if administrators think that one group of people will score the training lower than other groups or won't perform as well as another group, they may be inclined to dismiss or exclude the data *or* might adjust the scale to account for lower scores from a certain population.

Likewise, if administrators don't believe in the validity or impact of the training being evaluated, they could dismiss or exclude the data *or* might adjust the scale to account for lower scores.

Emotional Bias

Emotional bias affects Level 1 evaluation (reaction or smile sheets) to the greatest extent. This bias occurs when participants allow their feelings (like or dislike) for the facilitator to sway their ratings. Like and dislike are emotions directed toward an object or a person. In this case, the object of the like or dislike could be the program or the facilitator. If these emotions go unchecked, they may contaminate the ratings.

This type of bias is difficult to address. One action a facilitator can take is to provide interim evaluations to allow participants to express themselves. An overtly biased perspective (positive or negative) could then be addressed during the training course.

Restriction of Range or Range Error

Some respondents to a survey or questionnaire may engage in the error of restriction of range. This error occurs when respondents, or raters, restrict all their ratings to a small section of the rating scale. This restriction could be positive (leniency) or negative (severity).

In some cases, this phenomenon is an unconscious bias on the part of the rater. In other cases, the rater may like (or dislike) going to training. If the rater is required to attend the training, that could lead to a restriction of range on the negative side. These issues can be addressed when the evaluation instrument is being completed. If the evaluation is taking place with participants present, the trainer can have a brief discussion about this issue. The trainer could also include a brief discussion about these rater errors in the evaluation instrument's instruction section.

Rights of Human Subjects

After an instrument has been created, some administrative guidelines can improve the effectiveness of the data collection method, including protecting the confidentiality and privacy of data and respondents and protecting the data and its proprietary nature. These are some of the administrative guidelines:

- *Keep responses anonymous:* Anonymous feedback is highly recommended. It allows participants to be open with comments that can be helpful and constructive. Otherwise, input can be extremely biased and perhaps stifled because of concern about reactions from the facilitator or management reviewing the findings.

- *Have a neutral person collect feedback forms:* In addition to anonymous responses, having a neutral person collect feedback questionnaires is helpful. In some organizations, the program coordinator or sponsor conducts the evaluation at the end, independent of the facilitator. This method increases objectivity of the input and decreases the likelihood of the instructor or facilitator reacting unfavorably to criticism in the feedback.

- *Explain the purpose of the evaluation:* The facilitator (or coordinator) should tell participants why feedback is needed and how it will be used. Although this information is sometimes understood, it's best to repeat where the feedback goes and how it's used in the organization. There is still some mystery surrounding the use of feedback data. Restating the process in terms of the flow and use of data can help clarify this issue.

Tools for Problem Identification

Several tools are available to identify problems prior to evaluating and measuring learning. These tools include Lewin's forcefield analysis, cause-and-effect (also known as Ishikawa or fishbone) analysis, and hypothesis testing.

Forcefield Analysis

Kurt Lewin (1890–1947) is sometimes called the grandfather of organization development because of his profound effect on the field. His forcefield analysis helps identify the forces maintaining the status quo and helps clarify approaches needed to facilitate change. Forces may be people, traditions, beliefs, norms of behavior, political or economic conditions, technology, or other factors that play a positive or negative role in the organization development effort. Lewin identified the positive change forces as "driving forces" and the negative ones as "resisting forces" that maintain the status quo (see Figure 3-2). After the driving and resisting forces are identified, ways to eliminate or weaken resisting forces and strengthen or add driving forces are determined. Lewin believed that strengthening driving forces is often easier and more productive than eliminating resisting forces.

Figure 3-2. Lewin's Forcefield Analysis

Source: Shaffer (1988).

Cause-and-Effect Analysis

A cause-and-effect diagram is used to identify, explore, and display the possible causes for variation. It's also called a fishbone diagram because of its shape. The cause-and-effect diagram was developed by Kaoru Ishikawa, so it's sometimes called an Ishikawa diagram (see Figure 3-3).

To construct a cause-and-effect diagram, a clear problem statement should be developed and placed in a box to the right. Major cause categories are placed at the end of a main branch, or "bone." Any inputs to a process are often good choices. Next, the diagram is completed by filling in the causes. A question to keep asking is "Why does it happen?" Each "why" should be listed as branches off the major causes. Cause-and-effect analysis is an excellent tool to discourage practitioners from letting their experience as WLP professionals bias their perspective.

Figure 3-3. An Example of an Ishikawa Diagram

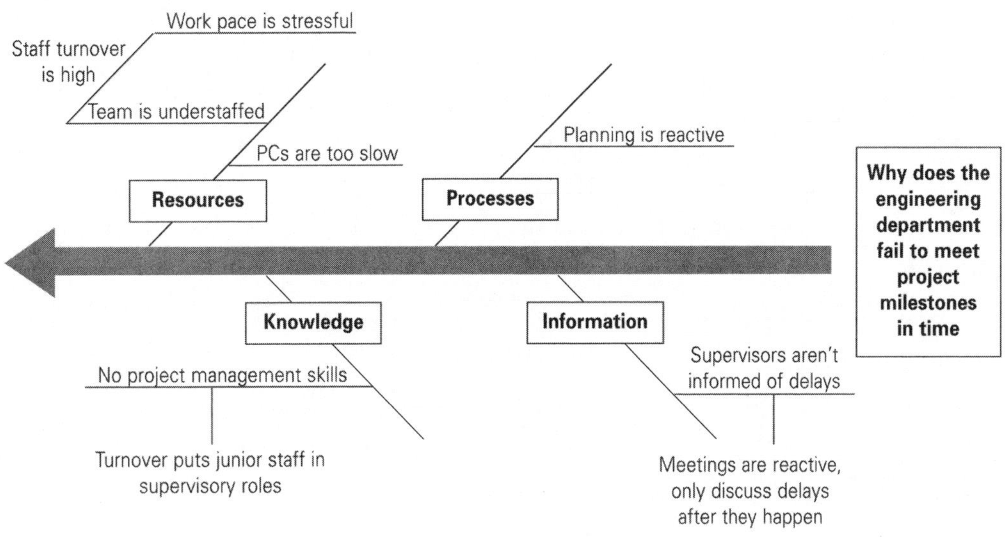

Source: Willmore (2004)

Hypothesis Testing

As discussed previously, the purpose of inferential statistics is to test a (null) hypothesis and then accept or reject the hypothesis. Generally speaking, practitioners should always test a null hypothesis—stating that they expect no difference between the treatment group and the control group. For more information on hypothesis testing, see the "Statistical Inference and Hypothesis Testing" section in Chapter 2.

Preparation for Research Design Development

Training and development professionals use evaluation data to ensure that their training or performance improvement programs meet the needs of learners and client organizations. Yet much of this valuable data is never used in any significant way to enhance the performance of learners or organizations. Focusing attention on the planning phase of the evaluation process and defining the future use of data will prevent this oversight and yield important training and organizational benefits. A comprehensive plan defines the what, why, how, and who of the evaluation planning and implementation process. These eight steps ensure comprehensive evaluation planning:

1. ***Determine the purpose:*** Pinpoint the evaluation's objectives to choose the right data to collect and to identify the right audience for the final report.

2. ***Determine stakeholders:*** The needs of critical stakeholders typically drive the evaluation's purpose. Four basic stakeholder groups are decision makers, program sponsors or clients, program participants, and training providers.

3. ***Determine the level:*** To select the appropriate level of evaluation, the stakeholders' needs must be considered first, which are defined in the program objectives in a front-end analysis. Another way to determine the level of evaluation is to compare the program with a set of criteria. The closer the program comes to meeting the criteria, the higher the level of evaluation to pursue.

4. ***Identify program objectives:*** Program objectives drive the evaluation-planning process. Ideally, program objectives reflect the stakeholders' needs and are based on a thorough needs assessment.

5. ***Plan data collection:*** Trainers should connect program objectives with each level of evaluation planned, describe the measures or data descriptors for each objective to define how to determine whether an objective has been met, specify the data collection method for each level, select sources of data, determine timing of data collection, and designate responsibilities.

6. ***Plan data analysis:*** Planning the process of analysis is especially important in Levels 4 and 5 evaluations.

7. ***Plan communication:*** Often a neglected step in evaluation planning, the development of a communication plan pinpoints issues that may influence the evaluation.

8. ***Develop a project plan:*** Project management is a matter of keeping a project's scope, schedule, and resources in balance and on track.

Data Collection Methods

The need for accurate information is critical in human resource and performance training areas to

- determine the current level of training in particular skills

- identify optimal performance levels and gaps compared with current levels

- conduct needs and training requirements analyses

- determine whether a course provided the required learning.

Before collecting data, a practitioner needs to determine whether any external definitions and standards exist for a particular question. For example, local unemployment figures may list clerical help as "typists," "stenographers," and "secretaries," but an HRD specialist's organization may use titles such as "word processor," "secretary," and "administrative assistant." In this situation, a difference in definition can skew analysis of the data collected.

The following sections examine several data collection methods and the advantages and disadvantages that practitioners need to consider when designing measurement instruments.

Simulations

Instructors' or managers' observations of on-the-job performance in a work simulation indicate whether learners' skills have improved as a result of the training.

Surveys

Surveys are paper-and-pencil, electronic, or email questionnaires that ask respondents a series of focused questions. Surveys vary widely in the amount of time and money they require and in complexity. It's important to choose the type of survey that will best provide the data needed—not necessarily the one that's fastest, cheapest, or easiest to do. Another factor to consider is whether more than one type of survey is necessary to collect different kinds of data about the same topic.

These are some of the most popular types of surveys:

- *Face-to-face:* This type of survey explores complex questions that require explanatory answers and is often used when asking highly sensitive questions, when all possible responses to an issue can't be anticipated, when respondents are experts or upper management, and when survey time and dollars are plentiful.

- *Telephone interviews:* This type of survey gathers nonsensitive yes-or-no or a range of like-or-dislike answers to specific, tightly focused questions and is often used as part of a training evaluation, when gathering strictly numeric data, when most or all possible responses can be anticipated, and when available time is tight and exploratory or sensitive questions aren't essential.

- *Written questionnaires:* This type of survey gathers broad, quantifiable, nonsensitive data and is often used in organizational assessments (when keeping respondents anonymous is important), when surveying large groups or a geographically dispersed population, when all possible responses can be anticipated, and when available money is tight and exploratory or sensitive questions aren't essential.

- *Electronic surveys (including email, web-based):* The use of email, the Internet, and intranets has opened many options for gathering information with written questionnaires. Software is available to post surveys on a web page or corporate intranet for respondents to complete. The survey can be completed online and often submitted directly to a database, thereby drastically reducing or even eliminating data entry. The survey results can be updated automatically after respondents complete the questionnaire, giving them immediate feedback on how their responses compare with those of others who have completed the questionnaire. Software is also available to distribute questionnaires via email. Respondents can then return their responses via email to a data entry person or directly to a database.

The following are the advantages and disadvantages of electronic surveys (see Table 3-1):

- *Advantages:* The most notable advantage of electronic surveys over mailing or faxing questionnaires is the rapid turnaround of responses. Also, after the initial investment to purchase software and training time to learn the software, the cost of survey distribution and analysis is minimal. There's no postage and often few, if any, data entry requirements because the software usually captures the responses. Many software packages also include rudimentary data analysis components, producing almost instant tabulations and graphs of data.

- *Disadvantages:* There are some serious disadvantages to using electronic survey software. First and foremost, many people in the target population may not have access to computers, email, or the web, or email addresses may not be available for all members of the population. Second, a significant investment of time and money may be needed to procure the software and learn how to use it. If adequate start-up funds aren't available or there's little time to launch the survey, the electronic version may not be the best choice.

Table 3-1. Electronic Surveys

Advantages	Disadvantages
<ul><li>They are inexpensive.</li><li>The results are easy to tally.</li><li>Participation is easy.</li><li>They provide quick results.</li><li>Frequencies (how many respondents answered a question each way) are easy to understand.</li></ul>	<ul><li>It's challenging to construct questions that obtain the desired data in a format that meets the desired needs. (Questions must be worded with care.)</li><li>The wording of a question must mean the same thing to all respondents (reliability), and the wording of the question must</li></ul>

Advantages	Disadvantages
• They can also be qualitative: Soft data questions yield qualitative data; the answer tally is quantitative.	produce the information that's sought (face validity). • Choosing an appropriate answer scale is critical. • Respondents can skew the results by simply checking all of one type of answer without really reading the questions. • Getting a large enough sample to make the data reliable can be difficult. • It can be difficult to ensure standardization of survey administration dependent on computer software or hardware.

These are useful points to remember:

- Surveys can be used to gather both qualitative and quantitative data.

- Surveys have various questioning options and rating scales, such as multiple-choice, Likert scale, and forced-choice questions. Two rating scales can even be combined for cross-referencing data.

Examinations, Assessments, and Tests

Examinations, assessments, and tests gauge what respondents know, can do, or believe in relation to the training being investigated. Types of assessments and tests include

- knowledge assessments, through verbal or written responses to multiple-choice, true-or-false, fill-in-the-blank, or essay questions

- actual performance of a job skill while being observed

- analysis of work results, product, or output against quality criteria.

Examinations, assessments, and tests are most often used to gauge current learner knowledge, skill, or performance levels. When constructing a test, it's critical to formulate questions and measurement criteria carefully to make sure they are clear to interpretation. An expert in test writing can ensure validity beyond pilot testing if the content is highly technical or if there are limitations in using other methods to corroborate the needs assessment outcome. In addition, as with surveys, a pilot of the examination, assessment, or test should be done with a small sample of the population to ensure face validity and reliability. Table 3-2 lists the advantages and disadvantages of examinations, assessments, and tests.

Table 3-2. Examinations, Assessments, and Tests

Advantages	Disadvantages
• They can be objective. • They specifically identify the gap between current and desired performance, knowledge, and skills. • The ultimate training design focuses on a specific gap rather than on generalized information.	• Assessments don't always get to the thought processes behind why a participant performed in a certain way. Accompanying them with an interview can yield more complete data. • Some participants can "freeze" and perform poorly because of test anxiety. • It can be challenging to include both knowledge and skill examinations, tests, and assessments because of time constraints in training. • Tests may not be constructed properly to withstand legal challenges about how the results are used.

Self-Evaluations

Participants can complete self-assessment tests or checklists to evaluate for themselves how comfortable they are with performing certain functions and where they need more remediation to ensure that they can complete tasks.

Archival or Existing Data

Archival or existing records, reports, and data—known as **extant data**—may be available inside or outside an organization. Examples include job descriptions, competency models, benchmarking reports, annual reports, financial statements, strategic plans, mission statements, staffing statistics, climate surveys, 360-degree (or upward) feedback, performance appraisals, grievances, turnover rates, absenteeism, suggestion box feedback, accident statistics, and so on. Table 3-3 lists the advantages and disadvantages of extant data.

Table 3-3. Extant Data

Advantages	Disadvantages
• It provides hard data and measures. • It can examine trends and patterns in data over time. • It has consistent	• Extant data is usually collected for purposes other than training assessment or evaluation, so training issues must be inferred from patterns in the data.

Advantages	Disadvantages
measurements that provide reliable data. • It doesn't involve employee confidentiality issues because data is used in aggregate form.	• There's no control over the methodology used to collect the data. • Extant data can be mixed in with data that's extraneous to the purpose, so it must be "sifted."

Data Storage

Several applications and solutions can be used to store and display evaluation data, including spreadsheets, databases, and tables. This section examines these data storage solutions as well as other implications for saving and storing data in a secure system.

Practitioners often design electronic spreadsheets to compile collected data into an informational database that can be used to analyze training programs from many angles. The good news is that after the spreadsheet is created and the formulas embedded, all the evaluator has to do is enter the data and print the records.

Using a computer application to manage data simplifies data analysis. Spreadsheet and database applications available on most PCs are suitable for this task. These applications often include

- a data entry table or form
- automatic calculations tables
- automatic charts for reporting.

Data Organization Methodology

Once data has been collected, analyzing and organizing them is the next step. This analysis and organization can be facilitated by using descriptive and inferential statistics and variance.

Statistics fall into three categories: descriptive, inferential, and graphical. As the name implies, the strengths (and weaknesses) of *descriptive statistics* lie in their ability to describe data. *Inferential statistics,* however, allow the user to make inferences about the data from the sample to a larger population. With inferential statistics (and a solid research design), the user can also begin to make statements of cause and effect and statements of relationships among variables. Inferential statistics are more powerful than descriptive statistics. *Graphical methods* for statistical data analysis have become feasible and more common with the availability of powerful software tools for portraying data.

Clearly, both descriptive and inferential statistics have strengths and weaknesses. The user needs to determine the application he or she is looking for and then select from the

Data Organization Methodology, continued

proper category. From that point on, the user must make additional choices to narrow down the alternatives to a specific statistic for a specific application.

Most practitioners use descriptive statistics regularly, whether they know it or not. Descriptive statistics are frequently used in conjunction with charts and graphs to provide an easy and simple way of visualizing trends over large amounts of data.

Variation, also known as *dispersion,* is another of the most practical statistical concepts; it is useful for summarizing large amounts of information. Variance combines all the values in a data set to produce a measure of spread. The variance (symbolized by S^2) and standard deviation (the square root of the variance, symbolized by S) are the most commonly used measures of spread.

Variance is a measure of how spread out a data set is. It is calculated as the average squared deviation of each number from the mean of a data set:

Variance (S^2) = Squaring deviation from the mean ÷ Number of observations

For example, for the numbers 1, 2, and 3, the mean is 2 and the variance is 0.667:

Variance = $[(1–2)^2+(2–2)^2+(3–2)^2]÷3=0.667$

Calculating variance involves squaring deviations, so it does not have the same unit of measurement as the original observations. For example, lengths measured in meters (m) have a variance measured in meters squared (m^2).

Taking the square root of the variance gives us the units used in the original scale, and this is the standard deviation.

Spreadsheets and Databases

It is useful to think of a data entry table or form as a log for entering all training evaluation results. The data entry table or form isn't used for reporting, so it's designed with the needs of a data entry person in mind. All decisions on color, fonts, labels, and overall appearance are geared toward making the data entry task as easy as possible. For instance, data entry fields should be white or lightly shaded.

As an example, in a spreadsheet application the first row of the data entry table (see Figure 3-4) identifies the basic course information and evaluation data sections of the table, while the second row contains the column labels for the rows that follow. Labels in this row include

- course title
- dates
- quantity of forms entered
- statements or questions from the form, one per cell, in the same sequence in which they appear on the form.

After the table is set up, the data can be entered, beginning with the course information. Then the total number of forms from the session should be entered. To enter evaluation data, all the ratings are added for each statement or question, and the sum is entered into the appropriate cell.

Figure 3-4. The Data Entry Table

Course Information			Design				Instructor		Facilities	
Course Title	Dates	Quantity of Forms Entered	Objectives Met	Topics	Pace	Exercises	Knowledgeable	Time Management	Seating	Comfort
Basic PC	Feb-03	7	31	29	25	32	35	34	35	35
	= SUM (5+5+4+4+5+3+5)									

Source: Kristiansen (2004).

This figure shows the basic layout of a data entry table. Note that the evaluation categories should follow the same design as the evaluation form. The labeled columns are visually separated into their categories by shading them differently.

Automatic Calculations Table

The cells in an automatic calculations table contain formulas that extract and calculate information from the data entry table. Each category column automatically averages the ratings according to the number of training evaluation sheets completed and by course. After the evaluator designs the calculations table, he or she doesn't need to do any more work to get average ratings for each category. The spreadsheet performs all calculations automatically. An overall rating for each category is shown in Figure 3-5.

This table is used to create charts. Note that the shading is the same as in the data entry table. This visual separation helps avoid confusion during data entry and analysis.

Automatic Charts

Analysis of data involves presenting data in various charts, including bar charts and line charts, to find trends. An evaluator can set up charts to automatically filter data and update data reports with current information. The ability to understand and draw meaningful conclusions at this stage is inextricably linked to the evaluation form's design.

Figure 3-5. The Automatic Calculations Table

Design	Instructor	Facilities
Sum of cells pertaining to design ÷ number of cells pertaining to design ÷ quantity of forms entered	Sum of cells pertaining to instructor ÷ number of cells pertaining to instructor ÷ quantity of forms entered	Sum of cells pertaining to facilities ÷ number of cells pertaining to facilities ÷ quantity of forms entered
Example:	Example:	Example:
$(31 + 29 + 25 + 32) \div 4 \div 7$	$(35+34) \div 2 \div 7$	$(35+35) \div 2 \div 7$
Design Rating = 4.2	Instructor Rating = 4.9	Facilities Rating = 5

Source: Kristiansen (2004).

Data Management and Security

Evaluation data should be kept confidential to protect the anonymity of respondents. For that reason, an evaluator needs to take extra steps in planning how long collected data needs to be retained, deciding on the means of naming spreadsheet files or databases for later retrieval, and determining how to ensure that the system storing this information is secure and that only practitioners who should have access to the data are allowed entry.

✓ Chapter 3 Knowledge Check

1. Which of the following is controlled by the evaluator when splitting groups into treatment groups and control groups?

   a. Dependent variable

   b. Independent variable

   c. Extraneous variable

   d. Randomized variable

2. Which of the following is an undesired variable that influences the relationship between variables that an evaluator is examining?

   a. Dependent variable

   b. Independent variable

   c. Extraneous variable

   d. Randomized variable

3. Which of the following is best described as planning and organizing an experiment to ensure that the right type of data, and enough of it, is available to answer questions of interest as clearly and efficiently as possible?

   a. One-way analysis of variance

   b. Sampling

   c. Experimental design

   d. Qualitative research

4. Which of the following is a characteristic of hard data?

   a. Anecdotal

   b. Opinion

   c. Attitude

   d. Objective

5. A sample should be a cross-section of the population with all characteristics of that population represented.

   a. True

   b. False

6. In which of the following sampling methods does each person in the population have an equal chance of being chosen for the sample?

   a. Random selection

   b. Random sampling

   c. Random assignment

   d. Random bias

7. Which of the following is the process for drawing the sample of people for a study from the population?

   a. Random selection

   b. Random sampling

   c. Random assignment

   d. Random bias

8. Which of the following sources of bias may be a source of measurement error when participants know they are being watched and evaluated?

   a. Sampling bias

   b. Observation bias

   c. Bias of central tendency

   d. Emotional bias

9. Which of the following sources of bias may be a source of measurement error because participants are hesitant to commit to either end of a measurement scale and just indicate responses near the middle?

   a. Sampling bias

   b. Observation bias

   c. Bias of central tendency

   d. Emotional bias

10. Which of the following identifies and categorizes forces into "driving forces" and "resisting forces"?

    a. Cause-and-effect analysis

    b. Ishikawa diagram

    c. Hypothesis testing

    d. Forcefield analysis

11. Which of the following is another name for cause-and-effect analysis and diagramming?

    a. Inferential statistics

    b. Ishikawa

    c. Hypothesis testing

    d. Forcefield analysis

References

Barksdale, S., and T. Lund. (2001). *Rapid Evaluation.* Alexandria, VA: ASTD Press.

Biech, E., and M. Danahy. (1991). "Diagnostic Tools for Total Quality." *Infoline* No. 259109.

Conway, M. (1998). "How to Collect Data." *Infoline* No. 259008. (Out of print.)

———. (2004). "Collecting Data With Electronic Tools." *Infoline* No. 250404.

Kristiansen, N.S. (2004). "Making Smile Sheets Count." *Infoline* No. 250402.

Long, L. (1998). "Surveys From Start to Finish." *Infoline* No. 258612.

McCain, D.V. (2005). *Evaluation Basics.* Alexandria, VA: ASTD Press.

Phillips, J. (1998a). "Level 1 Evaluation: Reaction and Planned Action." *Infoline* No. 259813.

———. (1998b). "Level 2 Evaluation: Learning." *Infoline* No. 259814.

Phillips, P.P., C. Gaudet, and J.J. Phillips. (2003). "Evaluation Data: Planning and Use." *Infoline* No. 250304.

Schwarz, C.J. (1998). "Mean, Median, and Mode." Available at http://www.math.sfu.ca/~cschwarz/Stat-301/Handouts/node30.html.

Shaffer, R. (1988). "Principles of Organization Development." *Infoline* No. 258812. (Out of print.)

Waagen, A.K. (1997). "Essentials for Evaluation." *Infoline* No. 259705.

Willmore, J. (2004). *Performance Basics.* Alexandria, VA: ASTD Press.

4
Analysis Methods

Analysis is the process of discovering and interpreting meaningful relationships in data and summarizing empirical results to answer specific questions about WLP. The objects of analysis can include but are not limited to individuals, workgroups, organizations, and functions. Specific analysis techniques often summarize the impact of programs or solutions, but specialized expertise is also applicable to a wider range of workplace measurement problems. Knowledge in this area should allow practitioners to explore data comprehensively to inform decision making and to balance methodological rigor and accuracy with feasibility and utility.

Learning Objective:

☑ Describe major methods for analysis to include ROI evaluation, cost-benefit analysis, utility analysis, and forecasting.

Uses of Analyses

Level 4 evaluation provides information about how change affected the business environment and influenced certain outcomes. Some leaders in evaluation separate Level 4 into two categories, as discussed previously— Level 4 as business results and Level 5 as ROI. The balanced scorecard approach presents a strong case that financial indicators (such as ROI) are important but provide a "rear-view mirror" picture of what's happening. A change in retention figures is seen long before it's reflected in the cost of labor. Therefore, financial indicators should be only one part of what to look for in Levels 4 and 5 evaluation.

One benefit of using both a business result and a financial indicator (such as retention and cost of labor) is that an evaluator can determine that, for example, an improvement in retention led to a reduction in the cost of labor. After conducting a Level 4 evaluation, the trainer would know whether retention played a significant part in the cost of labor. This data is important when designing large and expensive programs or when determining whether an expensive companywide change should be implemented.

Level 4 evaluation should be part of an evaluation strategy when tangible results are part of the products, services, and solutions a practitioner provides. The information sought in a Level 4 evaluation should determine business results and financial indicators—for example,

- reduction of waste
- decrease in time to proficiency
- decrease in errors
- decrease in customer complaints
- increase in sales or cross-sales
- improvement in customer perception
- decrease in product customization
- decrease in return calls
- decrease in days of inventory
- ROI, return on equity, or return on assets
- decrease in current liabilities or equity.

This level of evaluation relates to business improvements. Often it's these results that were the reason for implementing the program. Levels 4 and 5 evaluation help tie what was expected to what was realized and provide important information about whether the strategy was on track. These levels of evaluation should provide closure on a full-circle approach, starting with the business need and ending by quantifying the solution's impact on the business need. Table 4-1 demonstrates this approach by defining the business need and what needs to be qualified at the end.

Table 4-1. Preassessment for Level 4 Evaluation

Question Asked in Assessment	Question Answered in Level 4 Evaluation
What is the business need?	Was the business need met as desired?
What are the specific outcomes desired?	Were the specific outcomes realized?
What benefits should be involved in providing this service, product, or solution?	What were the benefits in providing this service, product, or solution?
What are the objectives?	Were the objectives met?

Business conditions, including the business environment or state of the business, are typically discovered when questions similar to those in Table 4-1 are being asked. Identifying these conditions helps identify the business value and can lead to determining measures. For example, if business conditions include a slow economy, a reduction in sales, and low turnover of inventory, the value may be in identifying cost reductions or perhaps in introducing new products or product enhancements to attract sales. The related indicators would then be costs or new product innovation and time to market. This is further demonstrated in Table 4-2. For Levels 4 and 5 evaluation, it's necessary to link these types of evaluation to the business measures or financial indicators.

Table 4-2. Identifying Performance (Result) Indicators

Business Condition	Business Value	Performance Indicator
High turnover	Reduce time employees need to become competent	Time to proficiency
High error rate	Make correct information accessible	Reduce errors
Customer dissatisfaction	Answer customers' questions consistently	Customer retention
Transaction completed too slowly	Make information available and easy to find	Increase the number of transactions or decrease transaction time
Reference material goes out of date quickly	Change reference material to just-in-time	Increase in consistent information Reduced errors

ROI Analysis

Ensuring that data was influenced by the change and not other factors is usually important when calculating ROI. ROI is used to prove that a training program paid for itself or generated more financial benefit than costs. There are numerous ROI methods to use when justifying or determining the payoff of a WLP solution. Three of the most popular are

- benefit-to-cost ratio (BCR)
- return-on-investment (ROI)
- break-even (BE).

Table 4-3 displays the BCR, ROI, and BE calculations used in this type of analysis and how to interpret the data.

Table 4-3. Example of ROI Calculations

Example	Interpretation
BCR = $\frac{\text{Total Benefits}}{\text{Program Costs}} = \frac{\$3,200,908}{\$277,987} = 11.51$	This program produced a tremendous ROI. For every dollar invested, $11.51 was returned, as reflected in the BCR. Note: The BCR is 1.0 when $1 is returned for every $1 invested. If the ratio is 0.85, it means that only $0.85 in benefits was gained for every dollar spent. In other words, the program lost money.
ROI = $\frac{\text{Total Benefits} - \text{Program Costs}}{\text{Program Costs}}$ $= \frac{\$3,200,908 - \$277,987}{\$277,987} \times 100 = 1051\%$	In terms of the ROI calculation, for every dollar invested, the dollar was recovered and another $10.51 was produced. Note: When a program's ROI is 100 percent, for each $1 invested, $1 was returned in net benefits. In other words, for each $1 invested, the $1 is returned plus $1, so there's a gain of $1. Benefits and costs are usually calculated on an annual basis.
BE = (Program Benefits for First Year x Life of Program in Years) – Program Costs	BE calculates how long it takes for the intervention to pay for itself. In other words, it tells how many years the program would need to

Example	Interpretation
	be in place and be used before it paid for itself. This formula is also called the *payback formula.* If a solution takes longer than three years to break even, it will probably be obsolete before it does so.

Often, a BCR is reported as being the same as the ROI, when in fact, as shown in Table 4-3, it is not. A benefit-cost ratio of 1.0 says that for every dollar investment, a dollar is returned; this translates into a zero percent ROI that says the program broke even, or the money was returned. A BCR of 2.0 says that for every dollar invested, two dollars are returned. This translates into a 100 percent ROI, which says that for every dollar invested, the dollar is returned plus one dollar. The return is that extra dollar. If there's a 105 percent ROI, one dollar is returned plus $1.05. If a 98 percent ROI is achieved (which is two percentage points below 100 percent), there's still a gain. A 98 percent ROI shows that the $1 investment was returned plus $0.98.

Utility Analysis

Evaluation can be a difficult issue because situations, programs, solutions, and organizations are different, and implementing an evaluation process across multiple programs and organizations is complex. Many evaluation models also have long formulas designed for specific, narrowly focused situations. For example, utility analysis measures a program's economic contribution according to how effective the program was in identifying and modifying behavior and, therefore, the future service contribution of employees. The Brogden utility estimation equation (Brogden 1946) can be used to estimate the dollar value of a training program, as explained:

$$\Delta U = N \times T \times d_t \times SD_y - c$$

In this formula:

ΔU = the total change in utility in dollars after the training program

N = number of employees trained

T = duration, in number of years, of a training program's effect on performance

d_t = true difference in job performance between the average trained and the average untrained employees in units of standard deviation

SD_y = standard deviation of job performance of the untrained group in dollars

c = cost of training per employee

This analysis is used to place a value on new skills, disregarding the actual impact of those skills in the workplace. Although the approach may be valuable and helpful, the task might be a bit daunting from the practitioner's perspective.

Forecasting

When mathematical relationships between input and output variables are known, a forecasting model can isolate the effects of training. With this approach, the output variable is predicted using the forecasting model with the assumption that no training is conducted. Next, the actual performance of the variable after the training is compared with the forecasted value to estimate the impact of training.

Steps for Creating Evaluation Instruments

The most difficult part of developing an evaluation instrument is determining what will and will not be included. Many data components can be assessed. In general, developing evaluation instruments consists of the following steps:

1. Determine the purpose(s) the tool will serve. Will it be used only for a certain type of instruction, and will it be used for WLP products, services, or both?

2. Determine the format or media that will be used to present and track results. Will it be paper, online, or both?

3. Select the items that are important for the business to track and that will help maintain the quality of WLP products and services.

4. Determine what ranking or rating scale will be used (Likert or a different scale).

5. Identify what, if any, demographics are needed (for example, length of time with company, position, department), but keep an eye on confidentiality. If the instrument asks for the position and only two people are in that position, confidentiality will be compromised. How will demographics be used for reporting purposes and data analysis?

6. Determine how open comments and suggestions should be captured (for example, as part of each question or at the bottom of the survey). How will open comments be reported or whether are they even necessary? What types of comments are outside the scope of the evaluation? How will they be addressed? For example, in a training evaluation, comments such as "no food provided" or "room too cold" are helpful but don't address the extent of learning.

7. Identify the degree of flexibility the tool needs. Will it need to be automated for use with web programs or computer-based training? Will it need to be adapted to other countries or languages?

8. Determine how the tool will be distributed (email, online, in person at the end of the program, in a post-project conference) and in what timeframe it will be administered after the event.

9. Determine how the results will be tracked, monitored, and reported. How will the data be graphed? How will raw data be used for reporting?

10. Determine how the results will be communicated to participants, users, and others. Will non-WLP professionals (senior managers, human resources director, and so on) have access to the information? If so, it will need a self-service component for delivery of results.

Some additional considerations when developing an evaluation instrument include

- The items and responses need to be quantitative and should provide little or no room for interpretation.

- The analysis of the items becomes more important because the instruments are less open to interpretation. Data discrepancies need to be identified and possibly researched. The analysis is more quantitative in nature and requires validation.

- Open-ended comment sections need to be validated with the anchor to ensure consistency and identify potential data discrepancies. In Level 1 evaluations, items should not be left open to interpretation. So, for example, in evaluating the courseware's content, a question may ask "How can the content be improved (more technical information, additional exercises)?" In this way the response is "anchored."

- Linkage between evaluation criteria and performance goals must be verified.

- The measure must reflect program objectives.

- The measure must be valued by top management.

- Enough data must be collected to enable reliable measurement.

- The measure must be free from known bias.

✓ Chapter 4 Knowledge Check

1. In calculating ROI for a project, which of the following is the correct interpretation of the data?

    a. When the ROI is 1.0, that means one dollar is returned for every dollar invested.

    b. When the ROI is 100 percent, for each dollar invested, one dollar was returned in net benefits. In other words, it paid for itself but made no additional benefit.

    c. When the ROI is 1.0, it indicates that it will take one year for the program to pay for itself.

    d. When the ROI is 1.0, it indicates that the training program was effective in modifying training behavior and the organization is receiving one dollar more in value from each employee who took the training program.

2. In calculating the BCR for a project, which of the following is the correct interpretation of the data?

    a. When the BCR is 1.0, that means one dollar is returned for every dollar invested.

    b. When the BCR is 100 percent, for each dollar invested, one dollar was returned in net benefits. In other words, it paid for itself but made no additional benefit.

    c. When the BCR is 1.0, it indicates that it will take one year for the program to pay for itself.

    d. When the BCR is 1.0, it indicates that the training program was effective in modifying training behavior and the organization is receiving one dollar more in value from each employee who took the training program.

3. When calculating the BE of a project, the resulting value is 1.0. What is the meaning of that value?

    a. When the BE is 1.0, that means one dollar is returned for every dollar invested.

    b. When the BE is 100 percent, for each dollar invested, one dollar was returned in net benefits. In other words, it paid for itself but made no additional benefit.

    c. When the BE is 1.0, it indicates that it will take one year for the program to pay for itself.

    d. When the BE is 1.0, it indicates that the training program was effective in modifying training behavior and the organization is receiving one dollar more in value from each employee who took the training program.

4. Which of the following best describes utility analysis?

   a. Is a model used to isolate the effects of training when mathematical relationships between input and output variables are known

   b. Measures a program's economic contribution according to how effective the program was in identifying and modifying behaviors

   c. Is used to prove that a solution paid for itself or generated more financial benefit than other costs

   d. Is used to ensure that the data influenced by a solution was not influenced by other factors

5. Which of the following best describes a forecasting model?

   a. Is a model used to isolate the effects of training when mathematical relationships between input and output variables are known

   b. Measures a program's economic contribution according to how effective the program was in identifying and modifying behaviors

   c. Is used to prove that a solution paid for itself or generated more financial benefit than other costs

   d. Is used to ensure that the data influenced by a solution was not influenced by other factors

6. For level 3 evaluation, it is necessary to link this type of evaluation to business measures and financial indicators.

   a. True

   b. False

References

Barksdale, S., and T. Lund. (2001). *Rapid Evaluation.* Alexandria, VA: ASTD Press.

Brogden, H.E. (1946). "On the Interpretation of the Correlation Coefficient as a Measure of Predictive Efficiency." *Journal of Educational Psychology,* pp. 37, 65-76.

Conway, M., and S. Thomas. (2003). "Using Electronic Surveys." *Infoline* No. 250301.

McCain, D.V. (2005). *Evaluation Basics.* Alexandria, VA: ASTD Press.

Phillips, and T. Hodges. (2004). *Make Training Evaluation Work.* Alexandria, VA: ASTD Press.

Waagen, A.K. (1997). "Essentials for Evaluation." *Infoline* No. 259705.

5
Interpretation and Reporting of Data

An important role of a WLP professional in the interpretation and reporting of data is converting the data so that it is easy for the general reader to understand. The process begins with selecting data and results to report. Translating data and results into an appropriate format for the intended audience may include ensuring that the chosen graphical format accurately conveys the information and providing supporting contextual material to place data and results in the proper context.

Learning Objectives:

- ☑ Define qualitative data.
- ☑ Review the principles for the visual display of quantitative information.
- ☑ Identify sources of estimating and reporting error and best practices for avoiding these errors.
- ☑ Discuss the issues involved with the synthesis of data.
- ☑ List the methods of communicating data results to users, and match each style with an intended purpose.
- ☑ List several considerations regarding the parameters for reporting information.
- ☑ Name the methods or media to communicate results to users and differentiate between each style.
- ☑ Explain the appropriate presentation of information.
- ☑ Describe potential influencing factors, limitations, and assumptions that provide a valid report of data.

Qualitative Data

Qualitative data is information that can be difficult to express in measures or numbers. Qualitative analysis involves looking at participants' opinions, behaviors, and attributes and is often descriptive. The data is typically collected through focus groups and interviews, although it may come from other sources, such as observer notes and survey comments. Often, personal perspectives and direct quotations are noted, and they can be quite wordy. The analysis identifies common theses and atypical data and categorizes data by specific topics.

Common sources of qualitative data are

- Level 1 comments
- competitive research
- best practices
- benchmarking
- any descriptive data gathered from people, including quotes, comments, and so on
- impact analysis
- observation notes or comments
- peer analysis notes or comments
- focus groups
- interviews.

Visual Display of Quantitative Information

After responses are collected, trainers need to tabulate and analyze them. Primarily, they want to use good judgment when analyzing survey results and should question results that don't "feel" right.

An evaluator should use charts and graphs to make the result of each question evident at a glance. The trainer should also use a cross-tab table for a pictorial comparison of results or two or more questions. (Computers are useful for this task.) Cross-tab tables can help analyze cause-and-effect and complementary relationships. For example, the cross-tab table between a question about age and a question about professional development might lead to a report that 20 percent of employees over age 50 want professional development opportunities.

Principles of Quantitative Information

The primary tools for quantitative evaluation are charts and graphs, and the two guiding principles for these tools are scaling and integrity. Scaling shows proportions and relationships. Integrity focuses on the presentation's truthfulness and accuracy.

In his book *Visual Display of Quantitative Information,* Edward R. Tufte (2001) states that graphics reveal—and should show—the data. The graphics

- induce viewers to think about the substance rather than methodology, graphical design, the technology of the graphic, or something else

- avoid distorting what the data have to say

- present many numbers in a small space

- make large data sets coherent

- encourage the eye to compare different pieces of data

- reveal the data at several levels of detail, from a broad overview to the fine structure

- serve a reasonably clear purpose: description, explorations, tabulation, or decoration

- should be closely integrated with statistical and verbal descriptions of a data set.

Estimation and Reporting of Error

Some data collection instruments have various sources of error inherent in the data. For example, telephone surveys and written questionnaires may have incomplete surveys and responses. An evaluator needs to decide what constitutes a completed survey, for example, answering 25 percent of the questions, 75 percent of the questions, or another specified amount.

If a computer is used to tabulate results, the evaluator should check for data entry errors, especially when the operator is entering the first responses. This check prevents the recurring errors created when the operator misunderstands a task. If staff is manually tabulating results, everybody should use the same tabulating system, and anyone tabulating results must understand the criteria for making decisions on questionable responses. Often analysis software can check for "out-of-range" conditions, that is, values that are far from the range expected and often due to a recording error. Paraphrasing should be done carefully so as not to change a response's meaning.

Another pitfall in interpreting data, identifying findings, and generating conclusions is evaluator bias. When a lot of effort has been invested in creating or supporting evaluation, it's easy to be biased about the results. Evaluators should follow these guidelines on good evaluation reporting:

- Be aware of personal biases and filter them from findings, conclusions, and recommendations.

- Be open to what findings say. Often "bad news" can provide creative opportunities for improvement.

- As data is reviewed, begin to generate options. This process stimulates recommendations and next action steps.

- Review the data from multiple perspectives. Put data in chronological order and then group it according to key events. Review it from multiple settings and demographics and do a cross-setting pattern analysis.

- If people are the primary focus of analysis, as in Levels 2 and 3, focus on their demographics and then interpret the data. For example, is there a difference in test scores between a manager and an associate?

- Organize the data by process. (For example, does the content support recruitment, and if yes, how?)

- Group the issues and compare them against other data findings.

- Analyze data from the perspective of a case study.

- Be aware of and change patterned ways of thinking and personal habits in viewing data. (For example, if evaluators are accustomed to entering data into a spreadsheet and then sorting it, they should try sorting it manually first and then entering it into the computer.)

- Make linkages. Evaluation is all about cause and effect. The data from an evaluation tool should have clear linkages to the business need, to the measures, to the content of a solution, and to the practice of WLP. Linkages should be identified and called. If they are missing, this is an important finding, too.

Synthesis of Data

Three major tasks are involved in analyzing data: sorting, tabulating, and comparing raw with summarized data. Regardless of the type of analysis, the process begins with sorting data by respondent type, location, or some other identifying information. Sorting data allows the trainer to see whether the information has been collected correctly. For example, if an online survey was used, it's easy to see whether each survey is completed correctly and what data needs to be excluded. Inaccurately completed surveys should be excluded from tabulation, as should incomplete interviews and observations.

Most inaccuracies in survey completion are caused by the respondent's misinterpretation of directions. Sometimes interviews and observations can't be completed because of some unforeseen problem at the time of the data collection; for example, the person being observed may be called away for an emergency or might experience extreme discomfort while being observed. Data from focus groups or job-mapping sessions, however, is rarely excluded.

Sorting results in data that's grouped for tabulation. Data tabulation, perhaps the most tedious task in data analysis, is the process of extracting and categorizing data from the instruments used to gather it; this process enables practitioners to review and understand the data. Data can be tabulated manually, by using a computer, or both. For open-ended data, such as that resulting from interviews or focus groups, manual tabulation is most often used in completing a content analysis, although some sophisticated and costly software is available that can perform this task. Sometimes a key word search is conducted with a computer program. The tabulation of closed data, such as that from surveys, is most quickly done by computer but can also be done by hand.

The goal of tabulation is to reduce data from its raw state into some type of quantified format without changing its meaning. Interpretation of data can't begin until it is tabulated and reduced. After condensing raw data, the trainer can compare it with the condensed data to ensure that the data hasn't been distorted.

After the condensed data is stable (that is, reflects the raw data accurately), it's ready to be interpreted. Several categories of analysis questions are listed in the following sections.

Content Analysis

- How can the data be coded so that it represents a category for data counts? For example, CP might refer to computer programs, or L might refer to leadership training.

- What is the meaning of the data, and what alternative meanings should be considered when reviewing the data?

- Is a reliable data pattern emerging, and if so, what is it?

Process Analysis

- What tools or support materials were used in completing the process? Was this use consistent across group members or specific to those new to the process or those with much experience?

- What variables affected the process?

- What interdependencies exist in the data identified for the process?

Quantitative Analysis

- What data discrepancies exist, and how can they be accounted for?

- What relationships exist in the data?

- How can the data be measured (for example, percentage, count, ratio)?

- What's missing from the data?

- What does the data mean? That is, how can the results be interpreted?

- What is the unit of analysis?

- Is the data reliable and predictable?

When trainers have finished interpreting the data and have the findings on the current situation, they are ready to list the results by key findings. The key findings enable them to take the interpretation even further by comparing the analysis results with the business drivers and needs that were identified.

Communication to Users

Communicating results is as important as achieving results. Handling communication carefully and planning it thoroughly is essential. The best process will be ineffective if communication isn't productive, specific, and performance-based. The skills required to communicate results effectively are almost as delicate and sophisticated as those required to obtain the results. However, to ensure adequate results, communication should be timely and targeted to specific audiences. The media used should be effective and the communication should be unbiased, modest, and consistent with past practices. Evaluators and trainers should consider communicating interim results so that the audience doesn't have to wait for the final report.

When communicating with key client groups, there are always concerns, for several reasons. Often communication contains sensitive and confidential information. An evaluator must safeguard this information at all times, and it should be very clear how it will be used and who will see the results. All communication should reflect a tone of using evaluation data and communication to be supportive, helpful, sincere, and timely.

An evaluator should carefully plan information presented to various groups around the needs of the targeted group. In some cases, the presentation should be brief and given at a general level. In other cases, it should be screened for confidential and sensitive issues. Still other groups need more detailed information. The evaluator must keep communication with client groups performance-based, focusing on specific issues, measures, behaviors, and additional items that reflect the nature of the training. An evaluator should always avoid unsupported claims and information.

Matching Style to Purpose: Synthesis Models

"A synthesis model is a structure, in words or on paper, that is used to organize and communicate a large amount of information—facts, ideas, impressions, attitudes, or opinions—about a subject" (Swanson 1994). Each of the eight types of synthesis models has different components to fit different situations:

- **Reflection:** This method involves thinking about data until a pattern, formula, truth, or metaphor becomes clear.

- **Two-axis matrix:** This method is used most frequently by analysts. One set of variables is a row of descriptive terms (horizontal) and the second set is a row of terms (vertical).Where the two axes cross, common cells are formed. Individual cells may be filled with information or may be void. Either condition should hold some significance for the analyst. A void that should be filled is a clear signal that an important piece of data is missing.

- **Three-axis matrix:** This model is a cube-shaped object used to express a set of abstract variables, such as judgments of quality, intervals of time, or types of things. The three-axis matrix is a powerful tool for breaking down and reconnecting a complex subject.

- *Flowchart:* This is a method for organizing and synthesizing information that contains input-process-output items, decision points, direction of flow, documentation or preparation steps, and confluence and divergence.

- *Events network:* This is a system-oriented synthesis model, used to describe and make visible what should be rather than what is.

- *Dichotomy:* This model is a way to approach ambiguous pieces of information by fitting data into two mutually exclusive groups, camps, or contradictory issues. Chris Argyris (1993) used this method when he subsumed management practice into two categories, espoused theory and theory in use, to show the contradictions between what managers said and what they did.

- *Argumentation:* This is a synthesis method aimed at resolving two or more theses or positions. Similar to dichotomy in that it explores two opposing facets of an issue, argumentation requires posing a best possible hypothesis and its supporting logic.

- *Graphic models:* Organizational charts, diagrams, and maps are examples of graphic models. These models make information visually appealing and easy to understand.

Use of Recognized Parameters to Report Information

When reporting information, certain parameters are followed, such as excluding the highest and lowest values if they are extremely outside the range and excluding suspect data (with disclaimers). It's important to state any known assumptions and bias clearly as well as any scale and labeling decisions. For example, when reporting weather temperature in the United States, degrees Fahrenheit rather than Celsius are used, or if the data focuses on monthly reporting, weeks should not be used as the timescale in a graphic. Another factor is whether the statistical model, method, or formula is usually applied to the given circumstances. If not, an explanation needs to be given for the exception.

Evaluation findings can be presented in a variety of ways; however, most reports usually include the following sections:

- *Executive summary:* This section is a brief overview of the entire report, explaining the basis for the evaluation and the significant conclusions and recommendations. It's designed for those who need only the most important information. The executive summary is usually written last but appears first in the report for easy access.

- *Background information:* This section describes why the evaluation was conducted and gives a general description of the WLP component, practice, product, service, or process being evaluated. The objectives of the evaluation are presented here as well as information about what was being evaluated and what it consisted of (for example, instructors, content, logistics). The extent of detail depends on the amount of information the report audience needs.

- *Evaluation methodology:* This section outlines the components of the evaluation process and identifies the tools used. The purpose of the evaluation should be identified and a rationale for the evaluation design provided. (The evaluation methods and instruments should be included as appendixes or exhibits). Finally, any other useful information related to the evaluation's design, timing, and execution should be included here.

- *Data collection and analysis:* This section explains the methods used to collect data. Usually samples of the data collected are presented in this section. Next, the data is presented with interpretations. If appropriate, the expected results are summarized along with information about the amount of certainty in convictions about the expected results.

- *Identified issues:* This section describes any unexpected issues or environmental concerns that arose during the evaluation. Other factors that might have affected the evaluation results should also be spelled out in this section (for example, the introduction of a new sales incentive program at the same time as the new sales training program).

- *Evaluation results:* This section summarizes the findings with charts, diagrams, tables, and other visual aids. The evaluation results section gives a complete picture of the evaluation's findings.

- *Conclusions and recommendations:* This section presents the overall conclusions, with brief explanations for each and a list of recommendations for changes, if appropriate, also with brief explanations for each. The conclusions and recommendations must be consistent with the findings.

- *Next steps:* This section identifies the next steps that should be taken as a result of the evaluation and the people responsible for the actions related to the next steps. The importance of this section cannot be overemphasized, as it's often difficult to motivate action on the recommendations. Outlining specifically what needs to happen, when, and by whom is a critical step in the success of an evaluation project.

Presenting Data

So how does a WLP practitioner take the data that has been collected and analyzed and interpret it to provide meaningful information for the reader? When reporting evaluation results, a trainer should

- highlight the key findings

- confirm what's supported by the data

- identify misconceptions

- call attention to what may be less obvious

- draw attention to key points that may not be understood or known but are important to the business need.

In developing the findings report, a practitioner should consider three key steps to present the data:

1. Match style to purpose.

2. Select the correct methods and media.

3. Avoid misusing statistics to influence a decision.

No matter which presentation method is used, the following guidelines help match the appropriate style of data presentation, including the

- level of detail of data, findings, and backup documentation needed

- business purpose of the evaluation with regard to key decisions the report audience needs to make

- how the results will be used

- prescriptive versus descriptive documentation and data presentation

- informative versus persuasive needs to convey information

- audience who will be reviewing the report and findings.

When deciding the correct methods and media to present the data effectively, the following elements are key factors:

- Executive summaries help quickly focus senior management's attention to the business purpose, cause-and-effect analysis, and findings.

- Oral presentations need to include time for presenting key data and findings as well as time for discussion among audience members.

- Detailed reporting prepares the presenter and provides reviewers with summarized data as well as charts, graphs, examples of evaluation instruments, and detailed information to convey the information at both overview and detailed levels.

Not Misusing Statistics to Influence a Decision

To ensure ethical behavior toward the client, practitioners should always approach the evaluation and instruments with an open mind. If they are trying to prove or disprove a personal theory, those desires bias the questions. Practitioners should also keep an open mind about the results. If results aren't what were expected and practitioners are not convinced of their accuracy, they should research to find out why. Responses that contradict the expected outcome should not be thrown out, but reported honestly and directly.

Providing Appropriate Filters: What to Present and What Not to Present

Making conclusions and recommendations and taking the next steps are where the rubber meets the road. Evaluation results need to be documented and decisions made and acted on. Some important considerations in this process are:

- Who needs or will use this information?

- What information is actually needed, and how can it be conveyed? .

- How will the information be used? What is the purpose of communicating the evaluation results?

- When and how often will this information be needed?

This statistical principle carries over to the reporting; the reader needs to be informed about anything that may have influenced the data. For example, a survey of the number of people eating ice cream should include the factor that the survey was taken outside, in Chicago, and on the coldest day of the year.

Limitations are another type of disclaimer. For example, a study done using only white males taking a standardized test is of limited, little, or no value for making statements about how black females would score on a test.

Determining Potential Influencing Factors, Limitations, and Assumptions on Data Sets

Assumptions are often made to use specific statistical models and principles. The researcher or writer needs to state what assumptions were intentionally made so that readers can determine whether they concur that the assumptions were appropriate.

These are some assumptions for the chi-square test for a single variance (Bluman 2003):

- The sample must be selected randomly from the population.

- The population must be normally distributed for the variable under study.

- The observations must be independent of each other.

✓ Chapter 5 Knowledge Check

1. Which of the following best describes an executive summary?

    a. It explains the methods used to collect data and typically includes samples of the data collected.

    b. It's a brief overview of the entire report, explaining the basis for the evaluation and significant conclusions and recommendations, and is designed for those who need only the most important information.

    c. It describes any unexpected issues or environmental concerns that arose during the evaluation.

    d. It describes why the evaluation was conducted and gives a general description of the WLP component, practice, product, service, or process being evaluated. The evaluation's objectives are presented here as well as information about what was being evaluated.

2. Which of the following is not one of the major tasks in analyzing data?

    a. Sorting data

    b. Tabulating data

    c. Developing spreadsheets

    d. Comparing raw data with condensed data

3. Most inaccuracies in survey completion occur during which of the following?

    a. Respondent's misinterpretation of the directions

    b. Respondent's lack of interest

    c. Respondent's skill level

    d. Respondent's opinions

4. The goal of tabulation is to reduce data from its raw state into some type of quantified format without changing its meaning.

    a. True

    b. False

5. Qualitative data is difficult to express in measures or numbers.

    a. True

    b. False

6. Which of the following synthesis models contains input-process-output items, decision points, and direction of flow to organize and synthesize information?

    a. Reflection

    b. Two-axis matrix

    c. Three-axis matrix

    d. Flowchart

7. Which of the following synthesis models was used by Chris Argyris and is a way to approach ambiguous pieces of information by fitting data into two mutually exclusive groups or contradictory issues?

    a. Events network

    b. Dichotomy

    c. Argumentation

    d. Graphic models

8. Which of the following is not one of the assumptions for the chi-square test for a single variance?

    a. The sample must be selected randomly from the population.

    b. The population must be normally distributed for the variable under study.

    c. The observations must be independent of each other.

    d. The respondent's opinions must be cross-tabulated.

References

Argyris, C. (1993). *Knowledge for Action. A Guide to Overcoming Barriers to Organizational Change.* San Francisco: Jossey-Bass.

Barksdale, S., and T. Lund. (2001a). *Rapid Evaluation.* Alexandria, VA: ASTD Press.

———. (2001b). *Rapid Needs Analysis.* Alexandria, VA: ASTD Press.

Bluman, A.G. (2003). *Elementary Statistics: A Step by Step Approach.* 2nd edition. New York: McGraw-Hill.

Long, L. (1998). "Surveys From Start to Finish." *Infoline* No. 258612.

Phillips, J. (1998). "Level 3 Evaluation: Application." *Infoline* No. 259815.

Swanson, R. (1994). *Analysis for Improving Performance: Tools for Diagnosing Organizations and Documenting Workplace Expertise.* San Francisco: Berrett-Koehler.

Tufte, E.R. (2001). *Visual Display of Quantitative Information.* Cheshire, CN: Graphics Press.

Appendix A
Glossary

Balanced Scorecard Approach is a model for measuring effectiveness through four perspectives: the customer perspective, the innovation and learning perspective, the internal business perspective, and the financial perspective.

Concurrent validity is the extent to which an instrument agrees with the results of other instruments administered at approximately the same time to measure the same characteristics.

Confidence Interval is the range where something is expected to be.

Confounding Variable is an unknown or uncontrolled variable that produces an effect in an experimental setting. A confounding variable is an independent variable that the evaluator didn't somehow recognize or control. It becomes a variable that confounds the experiment.

Continuous Variable is a variable whose quantification can be broken down into extremely small units (for example, time, speed, distance).

Control Group is a group of participants in an experiment that's equal in all ways to the experimental group, except the control group doesn't receive the experimental treatment.

Correlation is a measure of the relationship between two or more variables; if one changes, the other is likely to make a corresponding change. If such a change moves the variables the same direction, it is a positive correlation; if the change moves the variables in opposite directions, it is a negative correlation.

Covariates are the multiple dependent variables in a study with multiple independent variables.

Criterion validity is the extent to which the assessment can predict or agree with external constructs. Criterion validity is determined by looking at the correlation between the instrument and the criterion measure.

Dependent Variable is frequently thought of as the "outcome," or treatment variable. The dependent variable's outcome depends on the independent variable and covariates.

Dichotomous Variable is a variable that falls into one of two possible classifications (for example, gender [male or female]). An artificially dichotomous variable is imposed for classification purposes (for example, age classified as retired [>65] or not retired [<65]).

Discrete Variable is a variable in which the units are in whole numbers, or "discrete" units (for example, number of children, number of defects).

Effect size is a way of quantifying the difference, using standard deviation, between two groups. For example, if one group (the treatment group) has had an experimental treatment and the other (the control group) has not, the effect size is a measure of the effectiveness between the two groups.

Experimental Design is the process of organizing an experiment properly to ensure that the right type of data, and enough of it, is available to answer questions of interest as clearly and efficiently as possible.

Experimental Group is the treatment group; those participants who receive the "treatment."

Extraneous Variables are undesirable variables that influence the relationship between variables an evaluator is examining.

Extant Data is archival or existing records, reports, and data that may be available inside or outside an organization. Examples include job descriptions, competency models, benchmarking reports, annual reports, financial statements, strategic plans, mission statements, staffing statistics, climate surveys, 360-degree (or upward) feedback, performance appraisals, grievances, turnover rates, absenteeism, suggestion box feedback, accident statistics, and so on.

Formative Evaluation is an assessment done while it's being formed.

Frequency Distributions show the actual number of observations falling in each range or the percentage of observations.

Hard Data are objective and measurable quantitative measures, whether stated in terms of frequency, percentage, proportion, or time.

Independent Variable is the variable that influences the dependent variable. Age, seniority, gender, shift, level of education, and so on may all be factors (independent variables) that influence a person's performance (the dependent variable).

Inferential Statistics allow evaluators to make inferences about data from the sample to a larger population.

Interval Variables make it possible to rank order the items measured and quantify and compare the sizes of differences between them.

Intervention is another name for a solution or set of solutions, usually a combination of tools and techniques that clearly and directly relate to solving a performance gap.

Mean Score is the most robust, or least affected by the presence of extreme values (outliers), of the three types of central tendency because each number in the data set has an impact on its (mean) value.

Measures of Central Tendency are the three averages: mean (the average of a group of numbers), median (the middle of a distribution where half the scores are above the median and half are below), and mode (the most frequently occurring value in a group of numbers).

Median is the middle of a distribution arranged by magnitude; half the scores are above the median, and half are below the median.

Nominal Data are numbers or variables used to classify a system, as in digits in a telephone number or numbers on a football player's jersey.

Normal Distribution is a particular way in which observations tend to pile up around a particular value rather than be spread evenly across a range of values.

Ordinal Data are numbers or variables that allow ranking order of importance from highest to lowest.

Ordinal Variables are variables that make it possible to rank order items measured in terms of which has less and which has more of the quality represented by the variable.

Outlier is a data point that's far removed in value from others in the data set.

Program Evaluation assesses the impact of a training program on learning.

Qualitative Analysis involves looking at participants' opinions, behaviors, and attributes and is often descriptive.

Qualitative Data is information that can be difficult to express in measures or numbers.

Random Assignment is the process of assigning the sample that's drawn to different groups or treatments in the study.

Random Sampling means that each person in the population has an equal chance of being chosen for the sample. Choosing every tenth person from an alphabetical list of names, for example, creates a random sample.

Random Selection is the process of drawing the sample of people for a study from a population.

Randomization is a method that helps diffuse the covariates across the experimental and control groups. Researchers in organizations often have multiple dependent variables to deal with but typically want to compare one dependent variable with one independent variable (for example, performance in a training program—an independent variable—with job performance—a dependent variable).

Regression Line is the best-fitting straight line through all value pairs of correlation coefficients.

Reliability is the ability to achieve consistent results from a measurement over time.

Selection Bias is the error of distorting a statistical analysis by pre- or postselecting the samples.

Significant means probably true (not caused by chance) in statistics.

Skewness is asymmetry in the distribution of sample data values.

Smile Sheet is a nickname for the instructor and class training evaluation forms used in Level 1 evaluations.

Soft Data are qualitative measures are more intangible, anecdotal, personal, and subjective, as in opinions, attitudes, assumptions, feelings, values, and desires. Qualitative data can't be objectified, and that characteristic makes this type of data valuable.

Split-half Reliability is a type of test reliability in which one test is split into two shorter ones.

Standard Deviation is a commonly used measure or indicator of the amount of variability of scores from the mean. The standard deviation is often used in formulas for advanced or inferential statistics.

Stratified Random Sampling is dividing the population into constituent parts, and then choosing sample members randomly from the constituent parts. This method provides a more representative sample than the random sample. For example, dividing the population into age groups (10–20, 21–30, 31–40, and so forth) and then randomly choosing people from each age group creates a stratified random sample.

Training Transfer Evaluation measures the success of the learner's ability to transfer and implement the learning back on the job.

Treatment (Experimental) Variable is the term researchers and statisticians use to define the "manipulated" variable in an experiment. An "experiment group" receives a treatment (for example, attends a training program), and a control group does not.

Validity involves measuring what the practitioner intended to measure.

Variance is a measure of how spread out a distribution is. It's calculated as the average squared deviation of each number from the mean of a data set.

Appendix B
Answer Key

Chapter 1

1. Which of the following is not a key benefit of the evaluation function?

c. Determines the cause of the performance gap and appropriate remediation

2. Which of the following most accurately describes performance agreement and the importance of objectives when conducting evaluation?

a. Ensuring that every objective has a corresponding evaluation task

3. Which of the following best describes formative evaluation?

b. Assessing the effectiveness of a training program while it's in development

4. Which of the following best describes summative evaluation?

c. Assessing the effectiveness of a training program when it's completed and has been pilot-tested

5. Which of Kirkpatrick's four levels of evaluation evaluates the learner's ability to transfer learning on the job and usually occurs three months to one year after the training event?

c. Level 3

6. Which of Kirkpatrick's four levels of evaluation evaluates the learner's reaction to the training program and is usually administered at the end of the training event?

a. Level 1

7. Which of the following best describes a reliable instrument?

a. The extent to which an instrument is consistent enough that subsequent measures of an item give the same approximate results

8. Which of the following best describes construct validity?

c. The degree to which an instrument represents the construct it was meant to represent

9. Which of the following best describes concurrent validity?

d. The extent to which an instrument agrees with the results of other instruments administered at approximately the same time to measure the same characteristics

10. Which evaluation model focuses on cost-benefit ratio and calculating ROI?

d. Level 5

11. According to Tyler's goal attainment model, the objectives—the ends of instruction—are identified first.

a. True

12. According to the PBT model, learners must demonstrate knowledge or skills prior to leaving the class or instruction.

a. True

Chapter 2

1. Which of the following best describes a situation where the mode < median < mean?

b. Positive skewness

2. Which of the following best describes normal distribution?

c. The way in which observations tend to pile up around the mean, also known as the bell-shaped curve

3. Which of the following best describes dispersion?

d. Variation in values that could be widely scattered or tightly clustered

4. Which of the following best describes an outlier?

a. An observation in a data set that's far removed in value from the others in the data set

5. Which of the following types of data make it possible to rank order items measured in terms of which has less or more of the quality represented?

b. Ordinal

6. Which of the following types of data include the feature of identifying an absolute zero point?

d. Ratio

7. Variance is defined as how spread out a distribution of data points is, whereas the standard deviation is the measure of how spread out the data points are when the mean is used to calculate central tendency.

a. True

8. The reason that practitioners convert raw scores to standard scores includes which of the following?

b. To reflect where they fall with respect to the mean to allow scores to be compared and interpreted

9. An example of a relational study statistic that measures the relationship between two or more variables includes

a. Correlation coefficient

10. The primary goal of hypothesis testing is to test a hypothesis and then accept or reject the hypothesis based on the findings.

a. True

Chapter 3

1. Which of the following is controlled by the evaluator when splitting groups into treatment groups and control groups?

b. Independent variable

2. Which of the following is an undesired variable that influences the relationship between variables that an evaluator is examining?

c. Extraneous variable

3. Which of the following is best described as planning and organizing an experiment to ensure that the right type of data, and enough of it, is available to answer questions of interest as clearly and efficiently as possible?

c. Experimental design

4. Which of the following is a characteristic of hard data?

d. Objective

5. A sample should be a cross-section of the population with all characteristics of that population represented.

a. True

6. In which of the following sampling methods does each person in the population have an equal chance of being chosen for the sample?

b. Random sampling

7. Which of the following is the process for drawing the sample of people for a study from the population?

a. Random selection

8. Which of the following sources of bias may be a source of measurement error when participants know they are being watched and evaluated?

b. Observation bias

9. Which of the following sources of bias may be a source of measurement error because participants are hesitant to commit to either end of a measurement scale and just indicate responses near the middle?

c. Bias of central tendency

10. Which of the following identifies and categorizes forces into "driving forces" and "resisting forces"?

d. Forcefield analysis

11. Which of the following is another name for cause-and-effect analysis and diagramming?

b. Ishikawa

Chapter 4

1. In calculating ROI for a project, which of the following is the correct interpretation of the data?

a. When the ROI is 1.0, that means one dollar is returned for every dollar invested.

2. In calculating the BCR for a project, which of the following is the correct interpretation of the data?

a. When the BCR is 1.0, that means one dollar is returned for every dollar invested.

3. When calculating the BE of a project, the resulting value is 1.0. What is the meaning of that value?

c. When the BE is 1.0, it indicates that it will take one year for the program to pay for itself.

4. Which of the following best describes utility analysis?

b. Measures a program's economic contribution according to how effective the program was in identifying and modifying behaviors

5. Which of the following best describes a forecasting model?

a. Is a model used to isolate the effects of training when mathematical relationships between input and output variables are known

6. For level 3 evaluation, it is necessary to link this type of evaluation to business measures and financial indicators.

b. False

Chapter 5

1. Which of the following best describes an executive summary?

b. It's a brief overview of the entire report, explaining the basis for the evaluation and significant conclusions and recommendations, and is designed for those who need only the most important information.

2. Which of the following is not one of the major tasks in analyzing data?

c. Developing spreadsheets

3. Most inaccuracies in survey completion occur during which of the following?

a. Respondent's misinterpretation of the directions

4. The goal of tabulation is to reduce data from its raw state into some type of quantified format without changing its meaning.

a. True

5. Qualitative data is difficult to express in measures or numbers.

a. True

6. Which of the following synthesis models contains input-process-output items, decision points, and direction of flow to organize and synthesize information?

d. Flowchart

7. Which of the following synthesis models was used by Chris Argyris and is a way to approach ambiguous pieces of information by fitting data into two mutually exclusive groups or contradictory issues?

b. Dichotomy

8. Which of the following is not one of the assumptions for the chi-square test for a single variance?

d. The respondent's opinions must be cross-tabulated.

Appendix C
Index

A

Analysis, 17, 48, 52, 53, 61, 67, 70, 71, 81, 89
Argumentation, 83
Assessment, 69
Averages, 7, 24, 33, 61, 92

B

Bell-Shaped Curve, 28, 33, 37, 95
Bias, 8, 35, 41, 43, 47, 49, 50, 51, 53, 64, 73, 79, 83, 85, 93, 96

C

Causation, 23, 33
Confidence Interval, 23, 35, 47
Confounding Variable, 26, 91
Continuous Variable, 26
Control Group, 12, 15, 26, 27, 34, 35, 44, 46, 53, 63, 92, 93, 94, 96
Correlation, 6, 8, 23, 33, 91
Correlation Coefficient, 33
Covariates, 26, 27, 91, 93

D

Dependent Variable, 26, 27, 42, 91, 92, 93
Descriptive Statistics, 24
Dichotomous Variable, 26, 91
Dichotomy, 83
Direct observation, 13
Discrete Variable, 26
Dispersion, 26, 27, 30, 32, 37, 95
Distributions, 23, 24, 25, 92

E

Error, 7, 27, 35, 41, 42, 47, 49, 51, 64, 69, 77, 79, 93, 96
Evaluation, 1, 2, 3, 4, 5, 8, 9, 10, 11, 13, 17, 21, 22, 28, 39, 62, 66, 69, 71, 72, 76, 80, 83, 84, 85, 89
Events Network, 83
Experimental Design, 44, 48
Experimental Group, 26, 44, 91

Extant Data, 58
Extraneous Variable, 42

F

Flowchart, 83
Forecasting, 72
Formative Evaluation, 1, 10, 18, 95
Frequency Distribution, 23, 26

G

Graphic Models, 83

H

Hypothesis Testing, 23, 34, 38, 52, 53, 64, 65, 96

I

Independent Variable, 26, 27, 42, 44, 91, 92, 93
Inferential Statistics, 27, 34, 53, 65, 92, 94
Instructional Strategies, 3
Interval, 30, 92
Interval Data, 29, 37, 38
Ishikawa Diagram, 53

K

Kirkpatrick, Donald, 1, 11, 12, 14, 16, 18, 19, 21, 43, 95

L

Lewin, Kurt, 52
Likert Scale, 57

M

Mean, 7, 24, 25, 27, 28, 29, 30, 31, 32, 33, 34, 35, 37, 38, 44, 92, 94, 95, 96
Mean Score, 24, 25
Measurement, 5, 21, 28, 44, 49
Measurement Scales, 23, 30
Measures of Central Tendency, 23, 24, 25

Measures of Variance, 23
Median, 24, 25, 29, 92
Mode, 24, 25, 27, 28, 29, 37, 92, 95
Multimodal, 25

N

Nominal Data, 24, 27, 28, 29, 37, 38, 93
Normal Distribution, 23, 26, 28, 37, 95

O

Ordinal, 93, 95
Ordinal Data, 27, 29, 37, 38
Outlier, 27, 32, 37, 95

P

Performance-Based Training (PBT), 8
Phillips ROI Methodology, 15
Primary Trait, 46
Program Evaluation, 9, 93

Q

Qualitative Data, 56, 77, 78
Qualitative Measures, 45, 92
Quantitative Information, 77

R

Random Assignment, 46, 64, 93
Random Selection, 46, 64, 93, 96
Randomization, 27
Ratio, 30, 70, 96
Ratio Data, 30, 37, 38
Reflection, 82
Regression Line, 33
Relative Frequency Distribution, 26
Reliability, 5, 6, 7, 8, 93
Research Questions, 43
ROI, 1, 2, 5, 14, 15, 21, 67, 68, 70, 71, 74, 96
ROI Methodology, 1, 14

Appendix D
Case Studies

Proposed Implementation of a Client Relationship Management System

Australian Capital Territory Community Care

By Susan Pepper and Ronald Christie

A medium-sized Australian government agency in the health-care field identified a need for a Client Relationship Management (CRM) system that would assist them to bring some integration into their service provision. They established the overall cost for the multimillion dollar alternative and developed a business case, but had not been able to secure funding for the project. They then requested the Cyrene Group to prepare a projected return on investment on the initiative, which was to be submitted with the business case, in order to finally gain approval to proceed and be granted the investment dollars.

Background

Australian Capital Territory (ACT) Community Care is a recognized leader in the provision of community-based health and disability services in Australia. By continually developing its services to be client focused, the agency is at the vanguard of Australian community-based health and disability practice.

As a community-based service, ACT Community Care's 1,300 staff deliver services from 73 service locations, as well as client homes throughout the length and breadth of the Australian Capital Territory. The wide geographic distribution of staff and the diversity of the service offerings presents a range of organizational, logistical, and communication challenges.

At the start of the new millennium, the inability of its current systems to meet these challenges is limiting ACT Community Care's capacity to enhance and grow its services. For the first time it is threatening the agency's ability to meet its high standards of care and client-centered innovation. ACT Community Care needs to find a solution that will reflect and enhance its recognized standing as a leading provider.

The modernization of the ACT government infrastructure in 1999 represented the first step to a resolution of these problems by providing a robust and high performance wide area network (WAN) infrastructure. Despite this, currently only one third of ACT Community Care's 1,300 staff are able to use the WAN. The majority, who do have access, are administrative rather than clinical service delivery staff.

The agency currently runs its organization on a series of program- based "stand-alone" databases. There is no single client database. This promotes fragmentation in service delivery and in capturing client and service information, and does not allow ACT Community Care to efficiently deliver coordinated services to its clients.

Organizational Need

ACT Community Care has an opportunity to provide its clients with a modern client-focused information management system, which will enhance the delivery of health services and participation in government initiatives, while fully using the WAN infrastructure investment.

The CRM system will lead to significant improvements in ACT Community Care's capability through greater visibility of client needs, services, and general information.

It is proposed that an overeaching CRM system will deliver the following benefits:

- increase service delivery productivity

- provide coordinated and efficient delivery of client services and information resulting in better client safety

- provide ability to participate in government initiatives

- promote collaboration across the various programs providing services

- provide an electronic link between centralized intake lines and service providers, while meeting legislative requirements including maintaining client privacy and appropriately managing client health records

- assist clinicians in delivering modern health care

- allow accurate collection of data including minimum data sets to meet purchaser and national reporting requirements

- assist in the monitoring of service provision, outcomes, and community needs analysis

- provide the framework for a single electronic client record

- provide better client access and convenience

- reduce exposure to litigation

- prepare workforce management

- provide ability to manage contracts and growth

- provide ability to monitor outputs and outcomes, and proactively tailor service offerings to meet identified needs.

History

Since 1996, ACT Community Care has been trying to address the above challenges through participation in a multistate consortium for developing a Community Health Information Management Enterprise (CHIME). This New South Wales-led project has been beleaguered with time delays, increasing costs, and narrowed objectives. CHIME, a clinical- rather than client-based community health information system, still as yet undelivered, no longer reflects the dynamic and client-focused environment that ACT Community Care operates within.

Fortunately, ACT Community Care has been financially prudent in relationship to this project, having contributed a total of $200,000 to what is currently a $12 million project. Having actively decided not to contribute further funds, the funds allocated previously for this application by government ($2.6 million), including a recurrent funding of $715,000, are still available and are a potential source of funding.

Since 1996, the world of information management has not stood still and, in recent years, there has been a significant development in commercial off-the-shelf CRM systems capable of rapid deployment. These systems support client-focused processes, with a single database and intelligent workflow. They are designed for easy integration with other systems, in this case, specialized clinical systems and people management information (PMI). In line with the ACT government's service delivery policy, they support multiple communication channels including call center, Web, fax, and mail, as well as face-to-face service delivery.

The chosen system must be flexible to allow for quick change and expansion, reflecting the fact that ACT Community Care exists in a dynamic marketplace.

ACT Community Care has been prompted, through the issues with CHIME, the advent of commercially available CRM software, and government initiatives around electronic service delivery and information sharing, to reevaluate its current business and specifically its IT strategy. To this end, ACT Community Care has completed a business requirements document that focused on identifying current and emerging business requirements.

Feedback received from the 2000 ACT Community care customer survey reinforced the need for "client focus" and highlighted the importance of having sufficient information available, being treated as a valued customer, working with staff who attend to requests promptly, a reasonable waiting time for appointment, and ease of contact by phone.

Rationale

The rationale for the projected return on investment (ROI) for the CRM system is based on the following:

- The data collection process will assist in ensuring that all key stakeholders' and managers' client management reporting requirements are met in the CRM system.

- Through intensive interviewing with managers and key stakeholders, the process will provide projections on costs and benefits, which can be monitored and measured when implementation begins.

- It results in the design and development of a measurement and evaluation model for implementation;

- It will assist in achieving ACT Community Care's opportunity to provide its clients with a modern client-focused information management system, which will enhance the delivery of health services and participating in government initiatives, while fully using the WAN infrastructure investment.

With the above in mind, the key stakeholders and managers were interviewed to assess needs, objectives, and outcomes for a CRM system.

Expected Outcomes

The implementation of a CRM system and supporting infrastructure will meet the previously mentioned business needs in the following ways:

- It will introduce common business processes and share common data.

- It will allow clients to interact with ACT Community Care in a number of different ways and receive consistent information through the use of a single channel, such as phone, Web, fax, email, and so forth.

- It will focus on security to ensure client consent and privacy.

- It will enable ACT Community Care to gain full value for its investment in the existing infrastructure.

- It will improve information and reporting to enable better management of existing contractual requirements, specifically with respect to capturing minimum data sets. This will also provide better information to support management decision making.

- It will provide an open system that allows the agency to share information and participate in portfolio and government projects. These include the Health Information Network (HIN); PMI; integrated document management; and as part of Canberra Connect, meet the ACT government's objective to support delivery online by 2001.

- It will enable staff to respond to and deal with client needs at the first point of contact.

- It will allow common information to be shared electronically and to be accessible at all points of contact, ensuring appropriate and safe service delivery.

- It will allow ACT Community Care to understand the cost and risk associated with serving a client and proactively managing a client's care.

Evaluation Drivers

The events that precipitated this projected impact study are typical. The management and staff of the organization intuitively and instinctively knew that ACT Community Care had a series of major problems. However, in the initial cost-benefit analysis, they could only identify marginal savings over the length of the project. Consequently, the degree of savings had impacted their attempts to gain the necessary funding and, in fact, had constituted a significant delay.

Additionally, around the globe, there is more interest in measuring the impact of business strategy, including the implementation or proposed implementation of business systems and technology solutions and organizational change programs. Four major trends are driving these actions:

1. Programs are increasingly becoming more expensive to develop and deliver. The proposed CRM system is an example of this trend. Expensive programs require a comprehensive projection of benefits versus costs. An evaluation can determine

the degree of success the organization could achieve and the appropriate implementation methodology, which should be followed to ensure a high return on investment.

2. Within an organization, the importance of a CRM reporting solution, which assists managers to achieve business objectives, places the program at a level where accountability is required. Consequently, it must be subjected to an accountability review both before and after implementation.

3. Fueled in part by the success of total quality management (TQM), organizations are implementing additional measures to gauge projected success and monitor progress of the implementation against the projections. CRM systems are included in this trend, as they are measured, monitored, and evaluated.

4. Senior management, in an attempt to efficiently manage resources, have brought closer scrutiny to the distribution of resources and often require accountability for major programs.

Collectively these trends are driving the need for more accountability and evaluation in corporate programs.

Purpose of Evaluation

The proposed CRM system is an ideal candidate for a projected impact study for four reasons:

1. The CRM system targets a critical audience in ACT Community Care—management. It is imperative that current and future managers understand the challenges faced by ACT Community Care. By providing timely, relevant, consistent, and accurate information on client issues and services, managers will be in a better position to develop focused strategies, which directly align with business unit direction and service delivery.

2. The CRM system project is an expensive program to be undertaken by ACT Community Care. Expensive programs need to show their projected and real value; and a return on investment, in this instance, compares the projected benefits of the program against the projected costs of the program, which then identifies the projected rate of savings.

3. The return-on-investment analysis process identifies the commitment and ownership of senior managers for a corporate business solution. This process will also contribute to a cost-benefit strategy to shut down the legacy/renegade systems.

4. Projects, which involve key operational and strategic issues, often demand that appropriate measurements of success be developed, including return on investment.

The situation and issues surrounding the proposed CRM system made it an ideal project to explore a comprehensive evaluation. It also provides an excellent opportunity to demonstrate how to develop a projected ROI, so that the process can be transferred to ACT Community Care for use in developing future business cases and measuring and evaluating the actual CRM program development and implementation.

Objectives of the Impact Study

The study, designed to evaluate the potential success of a CRM system, has four key objectives:

1. to assess the impact of a CRM system in measurable contributions to the extent possible, up to and including the calculation of the projected ROI

2. to identify specific barriers and concerns about successful program implementation and use

3. to recommend an implementation methodology for the CRM system, based on the collective input of managers, key stakeholders, and senior managers in ACT Community Care

4. to detail the ongoing costs to ACT Community Care if no decision is made or if funding is not received.

Initial Key Issues

Several issues became apparent in the beginning of the study, which could influence the ability to develop a projected, specific, significant return on investment:

- The timeline for the projected impact study was extremely short and impeded the level of comprehensive investigation that would normally be carried out for implementing a system of this magnitude.

- There were no consistent business practices across programs, regarding client management information.

- Some business units/managers had no organizational client information reporting tool; therefore, they had developed or were developing renegade systems to support access to data in order to undertake their daily business.

- There appeared to be pockets of staff in the professional area who were reluctant to change their current practices for a number of reasons: they were frustrated, yet comfortable with their current systems and processes; they believed their roles were not administrative, therefore they should not be expected to enter data into a computerized record keeping system; they did not have access to a computer; or they were concerned about the confidentiality of clients' records.

- Perceptions of potential success are critical to the effectiveness of implementing a CRM system. Consequently, this study gauges the perceptions of the potential success of a CRM system from managers and key stakeholders. Often, perception is as important as reality.

Evaluation Methodology

The process normally uses a five-level framework; however, the levels of evaluation, as illustrated in table 1, can only be undertaken as a program is implemented or after a program has been implemented. In this instance, we have used Level 1 (reaction to the CRM system), together with the step-by-step ROI process model to ascertain the projections if a CRM system is to be implemented.

Levels of Evaluation

At Level 1, feedback was obtained to judge the reaction to the potential effectiveness and potential success of the program. While participant reaction questionnaires are typically completed at the end of the training, in this instance, reaction data was collected from key stakeholders through a series of interviews and questionnaires. We also introduced a data validation step in order to quantify data ranges and to identify any aberrations that may have occurred.

The validation method used provided an overall picture of the expected organizational savings, which were then compared to the aggregated savings that had been identified by the individual department directors and their experts. The total figures produced a mere 5 percent variance in the gross anticipated savings across the organization! The value of estimation using an agreed and rational approach had once again been vindicated.

Table 1. ROI process model: Five levels of evaluation.

Level	Measurement Focus
1. Reaction and planned action	Measures satisfaction with the program and captures planned actions.
2. Learning	Measures changes in knowledge, skills, and attitudes.
3. Application	Measures changes in on-the-job behavior.
4. Business impact (projected)	Measures projected changes in business impact variables.
5. Return on investment (projected)	Compares projected program benefits to the projected costs.

At Level 2, measures of learning are recorded to determine the extent to which skills, knowledge, and attitudes have changed as a result of the training and program implementation. In a CRM system, learning is typically assessed in observations, exercises, simulations, and objective assessments from the project faculty. Obviously, learning cannot be evaluated until actual program implementation.

At Level 3, on-the-job behavior change is monitored and measured. At this level, the evaluation focuses on what specific on-the-job applications have been identified, which are directly linked to the project. As with Level 2, Level 3 cannot be evaluated until actual program implementation.

At Level 4, the projected business impact of a CRM was measured. Table 2 identifies the key performance measures directly linked to the program, which were considered by the key stakeholders, with a view to projecting the business impact of a CRM system.

At Level 5, projected return on investment—the projected monetary benefits of the program—were compared to the projected costs of the program. This is the ultimate evaluation, as the true worth of the proposed project was determined by comparing projected benefits to the projected investment.

Data Collection Strategy

A data collection strategy was designed to meet each of the objectives of this study. The number and variety of individuals contacted for input and the variety of techniques used helped to ensure that adequate, quality input was obtained for the evaluation. However, the time constraints for the projected impact study impeded the level of comprehensive data collection and validation, which would normally be applied for a project of this magnitude.

Issues

Several key issues had to be addressed when designing the data collection strategy:

- Because a CRM system had not been implemented, data could only be collected at the reaction level. Nevertheless it provided enough information to develop an assessment, which progressed through the chain of impact to business measures. Data was collected in one process in the form of an interview questionnaire with key stakeholders and managers.

- Different types of data had to be collected to provide a comprehensive view of the program. That involved qualitative and quantitative data.

- To provide a complete assessment of the program, data had to come from a variety of different individuals so that different perspectives could be integrated throughout the overall evaluation. That strategy ensured a broad range of opinions, expertise, and contribution and enhanced stakeholder buy-in to the eventual solution.

- The data collection and subsequent analysis had to be objective. The individuals involved in the actual collection of data, that is, those from the Cyrene Group, were external to ACT Community Care. That helped ensure independence and objectivity as the data was collected, tabulated, summarized, and analyzed.

- Wherever possible, the data was reported so that the participants were not identified. That provided the respondents with an opportunity to be candid and open in their assessment and thorough and accurate in their feedback. Interviews with key stakeholders and managers were undertaken face to face; however, confidentiality was assured prior to the start of the interview.

Table 2. Linkage with key measures.

Indicate the extent to which you think your application of the various components of a CRM system will have a positive influence on the following measures?

	No Influence	Some Influence	Moderate Influence	Significant Influence
Productivity		22%	45%	33%
Internal customer response time		22%	33%	45%
Internal customer satisfaction		34%	33%	33%
Job satisfaction	11%	33%	34%	22%
External customer satisfaction	11%	11%	11%	67%
External customer response time		11%	44%	45%
Quality		11%	22%	67%
Cost Control		56%	11%	33%
Staffing, including: Absenteeism Staff turnover Workforce management Workforce profiling	11%	67%	22%	

There were very strong responses from all the key stakeholders, which suggests that the projected impact is very real.

Data Collection Plan

An effective evaluation had to be carefully planned with appropriate timing established and responsibilities defined. The data collection plan was developed by the Cyrene Group and approved by the executive director, corporate, and business development. The volume of data collected was high and comprehensive because of a CRM system, the projected cost of a CRM system in both time and money, and the target audience involved.

Timing of Data Collection

In an ROI evaluation the timing of collection is critical and would normally be collected at the completion of each phase. However, in this instance, as previously discussed, only Level 1 reaction questionnaires were collected via an interview as this was a "projected" impact study.

Although a CRM system is designed to have a long-term impact, the specific improvements are difficult to capture if assessed years after the program is completed. In this instance, the data was required to assess the potential impact of a CRM system for ACT Community Care. Key stakeholders and managers were asked if their estimates were based on first-year-only projected results or recurrent results. If projections/results were taken over a longer period of time, additional variables would influence business measures, thus complicating the cause-and-effect relationship between program implementation and improvement.

End-of-Program Feedback

The Level 1 interview/questionnaire is an essential part of any evaluation and is usually obtained at the end of training or initial implementation. In this instance, feedback was captured by the Cyrene Group during interviews with key stakeholders and managers.

The main topics covered in the interviews are shown in table 3. As previously discussed, the questionnaires focused on Level 1 reaction data and Level 4 business impact data.

Interviews with Key Stakeholders

Interviews with the key stakeholders and managers lasted about two hours. Each interview explored projected individual application and impact including topics outlined in table 3. Additional probing was used to uncover business impact applications and to gain further insight into skill applications, barriers, concerns, and important issues surrounding the success of the proposed program. Each individual was encouraged to establish a formula on which any estimates were based. That formula was validated and the interviewee was then given the choice of owning the estimate or withdrawing. In all but one case, interviewees were very confident in their estimations, and they could see that this method had real merit.

Table 3. Topics covered in the interviews for Level 1 evaluation.

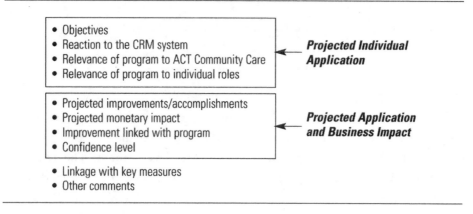

- Objectives
- Reaction to the CRM system
- Relevance of program to ACT Community Care
- Relevance of program to individual roles

Projected Individual Application

- Projected improvements/accomplishments
- Projected monetary impact
- Improvement linked with program
- Confidence level

Projected Application and Business Impact

- Linkage with key measures
- Other comments

Additionally, key stakeholders were also interviewed in relation to the ongoing costs and implications of maintaining the "status quo"—if no decision is made or a decision is made not to move to a CRM system.

Summary

Collectively, these data collection methods yielded a tremendous amount of data. The different perspectives and types of data ensured a thorough assessment of the proposed CRM system and provided a backdrop for insightful recommendations to ensure a high return on investment is received during and after implementation. We found that the estimation process was accurate and credible both in its acceptance and the results achieved.

Isolating the Effects of the Program

Normally, in this step of the process, specific strategies are explored that determine the amount of business performance directly related to the program. This is essential because there are several factors that usually influence performance data after programs have been conducted/implemented. The specific strategies used in this step will normally pinpoint the amount of improvement directly related to the program. The payoff is in increased accuracy and credibility of the ROI calculation.

While there are as many as 10 different approaches to tackle this issue, the options were limited with this evaluation because the CRM system had not been actually implemented and the various components of the solution had not been selected. The following strategies were used:

- Key stakeholders estimated the amount of improvement, which would relate to implementing a CRM system. With this approach, participants provided the total amount of projected improvement, and were asked to indicate the percent of the improvement that would be specifically related to a CRM system. In this instance, all of the projected savings were attributable to the CRM system.

- Managers estimated the impact of a CRM system on output variables. With this approach, managers were presented with the total amount of improvement and were asked to indicate the percent related to the program.

- Experts provided estimates of the impact of a CRM system on performance improvement. Because the estimates were based on experience, the internal experts were required to be familiar with CRM-type applications and how they could be applied in an ACT Community Care environment.

Collectively, these strategies provided an adequate adjustment for the critical issue of isolating the effects of the program as illustrated in the projection of savings (table 4).

The net savings are listed below by program area:

- Alcohol and Drug $110,300
- Child Youth and Women's Health $1,927,050
- Community Rehabilitation $897,860
- Dental Health $358,533
- Disability $1,633,768
- General Practice $46,298
- Integrated Health Care $2,125,200
- Corporate $371,300
- Total Net Savings $7,470,309

Validation Exercise

During the interview and after the above estimates were provided, we asked each program group three questions as detailed below:

- If the CRM System is implemented as proposed, what is your projection of the savings? Does this projection represent: First year only? First year and beyond? What is the basis for making the above projection?

- How confident are you that the above projection will actually be achieved? (100% = Certainty and 0% = No confidence)

- Other factors often influence improvement in performance. Please indicate the percentage of the above improvement/saving that would be directly related to the CRM system?

Table 4. Projection of savings.

Basis for Savings	Average Value in Dollars	Average Level of Confidence in the Estimate	Average Adjusted Savings
Common business processes and data	$2,832,000	75%	$2,050,200
Clients to interact with ACT Community Care in a number of ways	$ 607,750	74%	$446,688
Ensure client consent and privacy	$1,063,100	80%	$803,210
ACT Community Care to gain full value for its infrastructure investment	$819,500	80%	$655,600
To provide information/minimum data sets to support contracts	$849,273	79%	$726,868
Open system that allows the agency to share common data	$50,200	70%	$35,140
Enable staff to deal with client needs at first point of contact	$1,725,666	79%	$1,376,383
Allow common information to be shared electronically	$105,000	80%	$84,000
Allow ACT Community Care to understand the cost and risk associated with servicing clients	$1,700,400	76%	$1,292,220
Total Savings	**$9,752,889**	**77% Average Confidence Factor**	**$7,470,309 Net Savings**

Results of the Validation Exercise

- The validation exercise provided for savings in excess of $16,500,000 in the first year.

- All but two of the interviewees suggested the savings were first year and beyond.

- Subsequently, the savings identified from this method equated to $44,500,000 over the projected life of the CRM system.

- That savings compares with our estimated figures from each of the programs and broken down by objectives, which came to $42,500,000, thus validating the estimate process thoroughly.

- As this figure was slightly higher than gained in previous estimates (table 4), we used the lower figure for ROI purposes.

Converting Data to Monetary Values

To calculate the return on investment, data collected in a Level 4 evaluation is converted to monetary values to compare to proposed program costs. That requires a value to be placed on each unit of data connected with the proposed program. While 10 techniques are available to convert data to monetary value, the specific strategies and techniques selected for this study were as follows:

- Projected output data were converted to projected cost savings. With this technique, projected output increases were converted to monetary values based on their unit of cost reduction.

- Where employee time is a cost, the participant's wages and benefits were used for the value of time.

- Historical costs and current records were used when available for a specific variable. In this case, organizational cost data was used to establish the specific value of a projected improvement.

- Internal experts were used to estimate a value for a projected improvement. In this situation, the credibility of the estimate hinged on the expertise and reputation of the individual.

- Key stakeholders estimated the value of the data item. For this approach to be effective, participants had to be willing and capable of providing a value for the improvement.

Converting data to monetary value is a very important step in the ROI process and is absolutely necessary to determine the monetary benefits from the implementation of programs, whether projected or actual. In this instance, we tabulated program costs through the development of all of the related costs of the proposed CRM program. Table 5 contains the cost components included in the business case documentation.

The primary program costs pertaining to implementing a CRM system are reflected in table 5. While there is often some debate as to whether salaries and benefits should be included in the cost of the program, in reality, participants are not replaced while they attend training, and so forth; therefore, the organization does not experience a replacement cost. However, the employees are compensated for being on the job every day and they are expected to make a contribution roughly equal to their remuneration. If they are removed from the job, for say, two days, then the organization has lost their contribution for that time. To be fully loaded with costs and also to be conservative, that value should be estimated and included in

Table 5. Cost components.

Cost Component	YR 0 $'000	YR 1 $'000	YR 2 $'000	YR 3 $'000	YR 4 $'000	YR $'000	YR $'000	YR $'000
CRM application software	4,065	262	262	262	262	262	262	262
InTACT Support —CRM System	630	320	320	320	320	320	320	320
Database software infrastructure	492	252	252	252	252	252	252	252
Server infrastructure	623	624	656	688	720	752	784	816
Additional WAN infrastructure	461	245	245	245	245	245	245	245
Additional desktop peripherals	404	384	384	384	384	384	384	384
Commissioning— cabling, telephony, fit-out	701	0	0	0	0	0	0	300
ACT Community Care project team—Implementation	1,172	0	0	0	0	0	0	0
ACT Community Care systems support measurement and evaluation costs	381	381	381	381	381	381	381	381
Estimated Total Yearly Outlay	**8,929**	**2,467**	**2,499**	**2,531**	**2,563**	**2,595**	**2,627**	**2,960**

the overall cost profile. Cyrene Group worked on the assumption that these costs were included in the business case costing documentation.

Cost Estimation

ACT Community Care retained the services of a professional services company to assist in the production of a business requirements document. This process reveals a total estimated cost for implementing a CRM system as $27,171,000 over seven years.

Calculating the ROI

When developing the projected ROI, two important issues had to be addressed that represented a significant challenge for the process. The first involved the methods to isolate the effects of the program, while the second was converting data to monetary values.

The role of the key stakeholders and managers was extremely critical. The key stakeholders and managers provided estimates on proposed improvements, isolated the effects of the proposed program on the improvements, and in some cases converted data to actual monetary values. While there are many other approaches to isolate the effects of the program and a variety of techniques to convert data to monetary values, several issues prevented the use of a majority of other approaches and techniques:

- As this impact study was a projection, this fact alone eliminated some of the possibilities.

- The nature of CRM systems eliminated many other techniques. The application and ultimate impact is an individual process, and the improvements must come from the key stakeholders/managers themselves. Skills can be applied in a variety of situations to drive any one of dozens of business performance measures in a business unit. Given a cross-functional group, it is feasible for each person to influence different performance improvement measures as the CRM system is applied. This situation made it difficult to project linkage of the program to any finite set of performance measures.

- The number of programs represented and the nature of their issues, challenges, and performance measures made the process difficult to project linkage to any small number of applications. Consequently, input from key stakeholders/managers was often the most reliable way to identify the actual measure of projected performance improvement.

Challenges in Developing the Projected ROI for the Proposed CRM System

There were several challenges that were encountered as the projected return on investment was developed:

- The CRM system had not been designed and developed at this stage; therefore, the key stakeholders/managers were asked to consider the questions based on the deliverables being achieved.

- When faced with the prospect of estimations, some managers found it difficult to grasp the concept without prompting.

- In terms of estimations, ACT Community Care did not have any measures for productivity or quality, and some of the identified savings are potentially in these areas.

ROI Calculations

When developing the ROI, the conservative approach is to include only the program benefits that can be converted into monetary value and the program costs. The projected return on investment is calculated using the projected program benefits and projected costs. The projected benefit-cost ratio (BCR) is the projected program benefits divided by the projected cost. In formula form it is:

Projected BCR = Projected Program Benefits ÷ Projected Program Costs

The return on investment uses the projected net benefits divided by projected program costs. The projected net benefits are the projected program benefits minus the projected costs. In formula form, the projected ROI becomes:

Projected ROI (%) =Projected Net Program Benefits ÷ Projected Program Costs x 100

Projected ROI = ($42,489,555 - $27,171,000) ÷$27,171,000 x 100 = 56%

The decision to calculate a projected ROI was made to ensure that ACT Community Care implements a CRM system, which meets the needs and objectives of its key stakeholders and is funded accordingly. Because the objectives of the proposed program reflect bottom-line contribution, the calculating of the projected ROI became a reasonably simple issue.

Intangible Benefits

Perhaps the most important results of a CRM system implementation are the intangible benefits, both short- and long-term. By definition, these benefits are not converted to monetary value for use in the ROI calculation. They would not be measured precisely and are subjective, but are still very important.

Without question, the intangible benefits of this proposed program are real and significant. Most key stakeholders were able to identify intangible benefits, some immediately applicable, while others will be long-term.

Communication and Sharing of Knowledge

One of the most obvious and significant intangible benefits is communication. Without exception, key stakeholders and managers discussed not having access to client information across programs. A CRM system should significantly enhance communication and the sharing of knowledge across programs.

Summary

There are many other long- and short-term potential intangible benefits that relate to implementing a CRM system, which include but are not restricted to:

- enhanced teamwork

- enhanced and focused alignment between client needs and business strategy
- enhanced organizational image
- quality
- increased job satisfaction
- increased productivity
- reduced unscheduled absence
- reduced labor turnover
- reduced stress/anxiety levels
- improved customer service—internal and external
- improved customer response time—internal and external
- well-informed decision making
- improved staff morale
- full value for ACT Community Care's infrastructure investment.

Lessons Learned

Because this was a projected impact study, the lessons learned will mainly be gained at our post-implementation evaluation. However, one of the shortcomings of this particular case study was that we were severely affected by a very tight timeframe (eight days), and we were compelled to use the costings that were calculated by the professional services team. Therefore, we did not have the opportunity to validate these figures, and the customer understood and accepted this handicap.

Recommendations

The proposed CRM system was approved to evaluate on the basis of assessing the impact of the deliverables with key stakeholders and managers within ACT Community Care and using their feedback as input to developing a model for implementation.

The following recommendations were offered based on the collective input from key stakeholders and managers.

Recommendation No. 1

To move quickly and efficiently to adopt a CRM system as identified, because every day that is wasted costs ACT Community Care prohibitive dollars in time, people, frustration, and effective coordination of client service delivery.

Recommendation No. 2

In this environment of change, flexible, user-friendly methods are vital when accessing customer information, as opposed to the historical approach of cumbersome processes, paperwork, and structured reports. This requires a multipronged approach to implementation, which builds a solid infrastructure to support the CRM system. This approach should include:

- change management
- business rules and processes
- education—technology and content
- data validation and integrity.

All of these components should have been included in developing the costs for the CRM system.

Recommendation No. 3

If the future agenda is to revolve around "Enhanced delivery of health services and participating in government initiatives, while fully using the WAN infrastructure investment," then ACT Community Care must get the customer data right. This means ACT Community Care must know who its customers are across programs and what services they are receiving and requiring. A CRM system provides the solution to this challenge.

Recommendation No. 4

ACT Community Care should measure all major initiatives, which affect customer service delivery and human capital within the organization. The projected return-on-investment process highlighted the vitality and need for information to be gathered and assessed prior to a project being approved and funded. This methodology will also be vital during implementing the CRM system to ensure that the project remains focused, and the benefits, which have been projected, are achieved

Summary

Collectively, these recommendations would make a potentially successful program much more effective and provide a leading edge CRM system. At the same time, it would generate tremendous power for management and staff, while enhancing customer service delivery and human capital management in ACT Community Care.

Questions for Discussion

1. Do you think a CRM system is a good target for a projected impact study?

2. What extra validation steps could you suggest to identify additional benefits?

3. Do you think that the estimation process has significant weight in this instance?

4. What other methods/strategies would you suggest for isolating the effects of the CRM solution?

5. Would you accept that the impact study provided a credible projected ROI? If not, why not?

The Authors

Susan Pepper is the managing director of the Cyrene Group, which began operations in Canberra, Australia, in 1999. The company has three major target markets: human capital, business intelligence, and return-on-investment consulting. Pepper's background is in human resources, gained from a career in the public sector in New South Wales and from her diversified consulting. She has a passion for the strategic approach to people management and to the measurement and evaluation of all management initiatives. Pepper holds a business degree from Southern Cross University, Lismore, New South Wales. She has published articles on measuring ROI in the Australian Institute of Training & Development's journal and lectured business and MBA students on ROI in the Queensland and Canberra Universities. She can be reached at the Cyrene Group, 5/19 Ebenezer Street, Bonython, ACT 2905 Australia; email: susanp@cyrene.com.au.

Ronald Christie is the principal consultant for the Cyrene Group. He has extensive experience in consulting, which includes human capital, change management, and organizational development. With a degree in commerce from the University of New South Wales, Christie has developed a career through financial circles and has expanded his repertoire by working with a variety of public and private sector organizations. He has published articles on measuring ROI in the Australian Institute of Training & Development's journal and lectured business and MBA students on ROI in the Queensland and Canberra Universities.

Source: P.P. Phillips, ed. (2002). *In Action: Measuring ROI in the Public Sector.* Alexandria, VA: ASTD Press.

Tax Relief and Community Investment

The Commonwealth of Massachusetts

By William Hettinger

In 1998, the Massachusetts legislature passed the first act of its kind in the United States, an act requiring that the insurance industry in Massachusetts establish two pools of investment funds for the expressed purpose of investment in community development projects throughout the state. In exchange, the insurance industry was to receive relief from certain Massachusetts taxes. This case describes the process the insurance industry, the community groups, and the legislature used to create this legislation. The case also isolates the costs and benefits of the investment program and calculates the return on investment (ROI) to Massachusetts from the creation of this program.

Introduction

In 1998, the Legislature of the Commonwealth of Massachusetts passed into law "An Act Insuring Community Investment and Equitable Taxation of Insurance Companies in Massachusetts." The passage of the act was the result of many years of lobbying efforts on the part of both the Massachusetts insurance industry and the Massachusetts community development groups. What makes the passage of this legislation significant is that it was the first legislation of this type passed in the United States.

The purpose of the act was to reduce the taxes paid by the insurance industry in Massachusetts in exchange for a pool of money being set aside for community investment. With the passage of this act, Massachusetts had agreed to give up tax revenue paid by the insurance industry in exchange for an investment in its communities by the insurance industry. This was a conscious decision on the part of the legislature and was the intent of the legislation.

This case study will take the reader through the calculation of ROI to the Commonwealth of Massachusetts from the passage of this legislation.

Background

The name of the legislation, "An Act Insuring Community Investment and Equitable Taxation of Insurance Companies in Massachusetts," includes two concepts: the taxation of the insurance industry and community investment by the insurance industry. For many years, these two concepts had been independent. It was only in the years immediately prior to the passage of this act that these two areas were brought together. Initially, the insurance industry had been interested in a reduction in taxation, and the community development groups had been interested in having additional dollars available for community investment.

The interests of each group will be described, as will the process by which these interests were brought together in creating this piece of legislation.

There are two primary types of insurance companies: life insurance companies, which typically offer life and health insurance and annuities, and provide pension and retirements services; and property and casualty companies, which offer insurance for such assets as homes, automobiles, and commercial property. In the United States, the insurance industry is regulated at the state level. There is no national regulatory body. The companies are incorporated in one state and licensed to do business in many others. Massachusetts is free to regulate and tax the insurance companies doing business within its boundaries. Other states may do the same.

Massachusetts is home to more than 11 life insurance companies and more than 21 property and casualty insurance companies. There are many other companies, based in other states, which offer insurance in Massachusetts.

Throughout the 1990s, the financial services industry has been consolidating, and many insurance companies have been included in this consolidation. Several in Massachusetts have merged, been acquired, or moved out of state.

At issue for the insurance industry in Massachusetts throughout the 1990s were several taxes imposed on companies whose home office was in Massachusetts, but which were not imposed on companies that did business in Massachusetts but whose home office was elsewhere. Specifically, Massachusetts-based life insurance companies were subject to an additional tax on investment income that was not imposed on out-of-state companies doing business in Massachusetts. An insurance company receives a policyholder's premiums and invests these premiums to earn income while waiting to pay the claims on the policy. Maximizing investment income is an important part of an insurance company's operating strategy and directly affects the company's competitive position in the market. The imposition of an additional tax investment income by the state of Massachusetts was often cited as a competitive disadvantage by Massachusetts-based life insurance companies. Since the early 1990s the industry had been actively campaigning to eliminate this tax.

The Massachusetts-based property and casualty insurance companies were subject to similar tax burdens. Those companies too were subject to an investment income tax. They also were limited in their ability to deduct "retaliatory" tax payments made to other states. Retaliatory taxes are taxes imposed by one state in response to another state's taxation. In the case of the property and casualty insurance companies, other states would tax the Massachusetts-based companies in "retaliation" for Massachusetts' taxation of their companies. The problem was that the Massachusetts' companies did not get to fully deduct these payments from their taxes, and in effect were experiencing double taxation.

The tax burden was such that companies were beginning to consider location in Massachusetts as a strategic disadvantage, and they were beginning to consider other New England states as potential home bases. While this could have been considered an idle threat, Massachusetts had been recently stung when Fidelity Investments, the large mutual fund manager, had moved a significant part of its operations from the Boston area to nearby Rhode Island, partially in response to tax issues. It was beginning to appear that it was only a matter of time until legislature would be forced to remove the anticompetitive taxes and that this time was going to be sooner rather than later.

At the same time that the insurance industry was lobbying for changes to the tax structure, the community development groups began seeking additional pools of funds for community investment. With a decline in community investment dollars from other sources, notably from banks and government, these groups began looking to the insurance companies as a source of investment. The community development groups wanted the insurance companies to invest in the communities in which their insurance policyholders lived. There were two precedents for this request.

First, banks have historically had a mandatory community reinvestment requirement, mandated by the Community Reinvestment Act (CRA), which requires that they lend and invest in the communities from which they take deposits. CRA lending by banks has been an important source of capital to community development activities in Massachusetts and nationwide. The community groups wanted to extend CRA beyond banks, so that insurance companies were also included.

Second, in 1977, nine insurance companies had pooled some capital and formed Massachusetts Capital Resource Corporation (MCRC). MCRC was formed as a loan fund to provide long-term risk capital to the state's small and middle market companies and act to enhance the economic development of the state. By the mid-1990s, MCRC had established a successful investment track record and had contributed to the growth of many Massachusetts companies.

The first bill on insurance industry community investment was introduced in the Massachusetts legislature in 1991. That initial legislation did not get out of committee. Each year following this, similar bills were introduced in the legislature. None of the initial bills were passed. But the introduction of those bills did bring legislative attention to the issue, and the community groups continued to press for it. In the fall of 1996, the Massachusetts Association of Community Development Corporations (MACDC) issued a report, "The Insurance Industry and Low-Income Communities: A Failure to Invest," which was highly critical of the insurance industry's community investment activities. That report contrasted insurance industry's premium dollars from low-income communities with its lack of investment in these communities. The report was to become an effective tool for the community groups in developing legislative and community support for community investment on the part of insurance companies.

While the initial insurance industry community investment legislation had failed to get through the legislative process, by the end of 1996, the insurance industry had begun to be concerned about the passage of community investment legislation and the form of that legislation. The legislation that had been introduced now had more than 30 sponsors, and the community groups had issued a report critical of the industry.

The life insurance companies responded by convening an industry task force to study community development investments. They also hired Belden Daniels of Economic Innovation International, a Boston economic development consulting firm, as a consultant to help them sort through the many existing community development investment programs. In 1977, Daniels had been the architect of the now successful MCRC. The life insurance companies were beginning to examine how a community investment program might be structured. In the spring of 1997, the insurance industry task force issued a report to member companies on community investment programs and investment alternatives.

While this study was taking place, it was becoming apparent to the insurance industry that there could be a relationship between their requests for changes in their tax structure and the community groups' requests for community investment dollars from the insurance industry. The insurance companies were very interested in having their tax structure modified. The community groups and now the legislature were interested in obtaining community investment dollars from the insurance companies.

Once the industry task force had finished its work, insurance industry representatives began negotiating with the legislature and legislative staff on the form of insurance industry community investment legislation. While there was an initial reluctance from some parts of the industry to link the tax relief to the community investment programs, over the course of negotiations it became apparent that this approach could be of benefit to all parties.

Massachusetts State Senator Dianne Wilkerson held a unique key position in the negotiation and legislative process. As senate chair of the Joint Committee on Insurance, she would play a key role in any tax relief for the insurance companies. Additionally, her district included the Dorchester-Roxbury section of Boston, a community that stood to be a primary beneficiary of community investment dollars. Linking tax relief and community investment meant that the buy-in of Senator Wilkerson would be needed for success. Ultimately, this buy-in was received.

Negotiations continued throughout the latter part of 1997 and into early 1998. Several different structures were considered. By August 1998, agreement had been reached and the legislature passed "An Act Insuring Community Investment and Equitable Taxation of Insurance Companies in Massachusetts." (See table 1.)

Table 1. Tax relief and community investment key events.

1977	Insurance creates MCRC as a long-term risk capital fund for economic development lending.
1991	First insurance industry community reinvestment bill is introduced to Massachusetts legislature. This bill failed to pass.
1992-1996	Additional insurance industry community reinvestment bills are introduced to Massachusetts legislature. These bills fail to pass.
1996	MACDC issues report: "The Insurance Industry and Low-Income Communities: A Failure to Invest."
1997	Life insurance industry creates task force to study community investment. Report issued in May.
1997-1998	Insurance industry and Massachusetts legislature negotiate tax relief in exchange for community investment.
August 1998	"An Act Insuring Community Investment and Equitable Taxation of Insurance Companies in Massachusetts" is passed by legislature.
1999	Life Initiative and Property and Casualty Initiative begins.

Results of Legislation

The key provisions of the act were the repeal of the taxes the insurance industry wished to eliminate and the creation of two pools of insurance company community investment money, one from the life insurance companies and one from the property and casualty companies.

The legislation established specific hurdles for the insurance industry in exchange for the tax relief that was granted. From the tax perspective, the act removed the tax on investment income that Massachusetts-based life and property/casualty insurers had been required to pay. It also contained a provision that allowed property and casualty insurers to deduct retaliatory taxes paid to other states from their Massachusetts taxes. Massachusetts had granted the insurance companies the tax relief they sought.

From the community development perspective, the act required the insurance companies to establish two pools of investment dollars to be invested into community development projects in Massachusetts. Specifically, the life insurance companies in aggregate were to contribute up to $20 million per year for five years to a pool of funds that would be used for investment. Likewise, the property and casualty companies were also to contribute up to $20 million per year for five years to a pool of community investment funds. The contribution of each individual company is pro rata based on the share of the investment income tax they had been paying. In total, the insurance industry could contribute $40 million per year for five years, which could grow to a $200 million investment. (See table 2.)

The life insurance companies established the Life Initiative to manage their community investment programs and have housed the Life Initiative operations within the MCRC organization. The property and casualty companies have established the Property and Casualty Initiative (PCI) to manage their community investment programs. Together these entities are known as the Insurance Initiatives.

The legislation mandates that the Life Initiative and PCI exist for 24 years. The insurance companies can begin to pull out their invested capital in the 20th year, and may pull out one-fifth of their investment per year in each of years 20 through 24.

The operating strategy of the Life Initiative and PCI is similar. Their investment strategies will be tailored to match both their five-year funding period between 1999 and 2004 and their final payout period between 2018 and 2023. In between, they will make both long- and short-term investments, with the intent of investing their pool of funds five or more times.

Massachusetts uses July 1 as the beginning of its tax and fiscal year. Although the legislation was passed in August 1998, the tax relief did not become effective until July 1999, nearly a full year after the passage of the legislation. As a result, the first insurance company investment capital contributions to the Insurance Initiatives were not required until mid-1999.

Both the insurance companies and the Commonwealth of Massachusetts benefit from the creation of this legislation. The remainder of this case will be devoted to evaluating the actual results of implementing the legislation and will perform an ROI evaluation of the impact of this legislation to the Commonwealth of Massachusetts.

This ROI evaluation has been conducted to determine the impact of this legislation to community development in Massachusetts.

Table 2. Summary of legislation.

A.	Investment income tax repealed for life insurance companies.
B.	Investment income tax repealed for property/casualty insurance companies.
C.	Property/casualty companies may deduct retaliatory tax payments.
D.	Life Initiative and Property/Casualty Initiatives created to invest in community development.
E.	Up to $200 million to be committed to community investment for 24 years.

Evaluation Methodology

The Insurance Initiatives began operation in 1999 and have been in operation for almost two years as this study is written, so actual operating data is available for a limited period. Overall, the Insurance Initiatives will be in operation for 24 years. This evaluation will include costs and benefits over the specific operating life of the Insurance Initiatives. The value of future benefits and costs will be discounted to obtain the net present value of these future benefits.

Costs

The primary cost of this legislation is the tax revenue that Massachusetts gives up as a result of granting tax relief to the insurance companies. The two obvious questions are how many tax dollars did the state give up and over how many years could the state expect to receive this tax revenue? On the surface, both questions are difficult to answer, but through further research, it is possible to obtain conservative estimates for these values.

Insurance companies are required to file many reports of financial condition and financial operation with the state of Massachusetts. The first place to look for the value of the tax revenue is in these public reports. Unfortunately, these reports do not break out tax payments or investment income in sufficient detail to be able to obtain an estimate of the value of these tax payments. The information on the reports is too summarized.

During the negotiation process between the insurance industry and legislature, as the provisions of this act were being created, the negotiation team assigned a value of $40 million per year to these taxes ($20 million annually from the life insurance companies, $20 million annually from the property and casualty companies). The negotiating team used this $40 million number as the basis for the insurance companies' contribution to the Insurance Initiatives. They estimated the state was going to give up $40 million per year in tax revenue and wanted the industry to contribute a similar amount to the Insurance Initiatives for community investment.

Following the negotiations, the estimates of value of the tax relief increased. On August 11, 1998, when the legislation was passed, the Boston Globe reported "Acting Governor Paul Cellucci signed legislation that grants $48 million a year in tax relief to Massachusetts-based insurers...." The act contains specific references to $20 million life insurance company investment income tax, $20 million of property and casualty company investment income tax, and $8 million of retaliatory taxes, for a total of $48 million.

Forty-eight million is the more conservative estimate of the value of the tax relief. This value is validated in the most recent newspaper accounts of the legislation and is contained within the legislation itself. This conservative estimate of $48 million per year is used as the cost of the tax relief in calculation of the ROI from this program.

In the negotiation process, the negotiating team also assigned a five-year horizon to the tax revenue when they established a five-year pay-in period to the Insurance Initiatives. The appropriate horizon for the tax revenue is a critical part of establishing the costs for the ROI calculation. As was discussed earlier, the financial services industry is in the process of consolidation, and as this consolidation continues, Massachusetts can expect fewer and fewer insurance companies to be based within its borders. Because the taxes were only imposed on companies based in Massachusetts, they were a competitive disadvantage for companies located in the state. The threat of additional companies leaving the state was real. It is highly unlikely that Massachusetts would continue to receive the tax revenue at the current level for very long. The ROI has been calculated using a five-year horizon for the phase-out of the tax revenue, the period used by the legislature when creating the legislation.

While the cost of the tax relief is the primary cost of this legislation, there are additional costs. These are the costs incurred in negotiating and setting up the programs and the costs for the ongoing operation of the Insurance Initiatives over their 24-year life.

The negotiation of the legislation took place over a 16-month period, from the spring of 1997 through August 1998. The negotiation process involved representatives from the insurance industry, representatives from the legislature, and outside attorneys. While the negotiation period was more than a year, actual time devoted to negotiations was under a month. Out-of-pocket costs were incurred by the insurance industry for outside attorneys. Other negotiators were legislative representatives and legislative staff, and staff from the insurance companies and their trade groups. Based on the negotiation time and level of staff and representatives required, the cost of negotiation is estimated at $288,000.

The legislation resulted in the creation of two organizations, the Life Initiative and PCI. The Life Initiative has been housed within the existing MCRC organization, while a new organization was created for PCI. The Life Initiative has hired a staff of three, two professional level people and an administrative person. Likewise, PCI has also hired two professional level people and one administrative person. The Life Initiative has located its offices within MCRC, sharing existing office space in MCRC's downtown Boston offices. PCI has rented space from a nonprofit agency in the Dorchester section of Boston. Staff and office space are the primary expenses of the organizations. In addition, the organizations incur costs for travel throughout the state and for outreach to the community and community groups. Overall, the annual costs of operation for the two organizations have been estimated at $700,000 per year. This conservative estimate of operating costs has been used because the organizations have only been operating for two years, and actual operating costs have not been published. An inflation factor of 2.5 percent has been applied to operating costs for future years. Overall, it is estimated to cost more than $22 million to operate the Insurance Initiatives over their 24-year life.

The organizations are structured such that the money for operating costs comes from the income earned on the investments. The community development projects pay interest to the Insurance Initiatives for the use of their money. The interest from these investments is used to pay the operating costs of the initiatives, with the remainder being paid to the participating insurance companies. (See table 3.)

Benefits

The objective of the legislation was that the Life Initiative and PCI each be capitalized with $100 million for community investment, for a total of $200 million. The funds would have a life of 24 years. The money would be deposited to these funds over the first five years, principal capital repaid from maturing investments would be reinvested in additional community development projects through the 19th year, and the insurance companies would be able to take their capital investment back in years 20 through 24.

Investment by an insurance company is optional. A company that contributes to the Life Initiative or PCI is eligible for the associated tax relief based on the amount of its contribution. A company that does not contribute is not eligible for tax relief.

While it was expected at the time the legislation was passed that a total of $200 million would be invested, the November 2000 report, "Insuring the Future of Our Communities: The First Progress Report on the Massachusetts Insurance Industry Investment Initiatives" prepared by the Massachusetts Association of Community Development Corporations, estimates that the total investment will equal $181 million, $19 million short of the expected investment amount. This short fall is due primarily to property and casualty insurance companies not investing in PCI at the level anticipated. Table 4 shows the investment by year.

Before the value of the Insurance Initiatives can be calculated, the money available for investment must be adjusted for credit losses. That is, the pool of funds must be adjusted for money that is invested but is not repaid. For the ROI calculation, a credit loss factor of 10 percent over the life of the Initiatives has been assumed. This means that over time, 10 percent of the principal invested will not be repaid. Ten percent represents a conservative estimate of the credit loss factor.

Other community investment organizations and financial intermediaries that lend money in a manner similar to the Insurance Initiatives have credit loss factors ranging from 2.5 percent to 10 percent, with most being below 5 percent over time.

Table 3. Costs.

Year	Cost of Tax Relief	Initial Fund Cost	Cost of Fund Operation	Total Annual Cost
1	$48,000,000	$288,000	$700,000	$48,988,000
2	48,000,000		717,500	48,717,500
3	48,000,000		735,438	48,735,438
4	48,000,000		753,823	48,753,823
5	48,000,000		772,669	48,772,669
6			791,986	791,986
7			811,785	811,785
8			832,080	832,080
9			852,882	852,882
10			874,204	874,204
11			896,059	896,059
12			918,461	918,461
13			941,422	941,422
14			964,958	964,958
15			989,082	989,082
16			1,013,809	1,013,809
17			1,039,154	1,039,154
18			1,065,133	1,065,133
19			1,091,761	1,091,761
20			1,119,055	1,119,055
21			1,147,032	1,147,032
22			1,175,707	1,175,707
23			1,205,100	1,205,100
24			1,235,227	1,235,227
Total	**$240,000,000**	**$288,000**	**$22,644,327**	**$262,932,327**

Table 4. Investment into insurance initiatives.

Year	Life Company Investment	Property/Casualty Company Investment	Total Investment
1999	$19,900,000	$16,348,800	$36,248,800
2000	19,900,000	16,348,800	36,248,800
2001	19,968,800	16,348,800	36,317,600
2002	20,000,000	16,348,800	36,348,800
2003	20,000,000	16,348,800	36,348,800
Total	**$99,768,800**	**$81,744,000**	**$181,512,800**

A key benefit to community development activities in Massachusetts from the Insurance Initiatives is that principal capital repaid from maturing investments will be reinvested into additional community development projects throughout the life of the Initiatives. The Insurance Initiatives are making short-term, intermediate-term, and long-term investments. Short-term investments are under three years. Intermediate-term investments are between three and seven years, and long-term investments are beyond seven years. Because the insurance companies cannot begin to pull their capital out until the beginning of the 19th year, the capital in the funds can be reinvested. As the shorter-term investments mature, the investment capital is returned to the Initiatives, and then reinvested in additional community development projects. Rufus Phillips, vice president of PCI, estimates that PCI will attempt to turn over the investment funds four or five times during the 24-year life. The Life Initiative is expected do the same. That means that the $181 million could be used to generate $724 million of community investments, assuming a turnover rate of four times.

The November 2000 report by the Massachusetts Association of Community Development Corporations provides a more conservative estimate. The Life Initiative, based on its first two years of investments (approximately $40 million), estimates $5 million of repayments available for reinvestment in year six. Translated over the entire $100 million Life Initiative investment pool, this would be $12.5 million of repayment available for reinvestment in year six. This translates to 12.5 percent of the capital being available for reinvestment in each year, from which a 2.6 times turnover rate can be calculated. With a turnover rate of 2.6 times, the $181 million would generate $470 million of community development investment over 20 years. The more conservative 2.6 times turnover rate for the investment funds has been used in the calculation of benefits for the ROI calculation. Table 5 provides a summary of funds available for investment. Table 6 shows the calculation of the turnover rate.

ROI Calculation

Once the costs and benefits have been determined, the next step is the calculation of the net present value (NPV) of the costs and benefits. The annual benefit and cost amounts have been determined as described above. Benefits include the initial investment into the Insurance Initiatives by the insurance companies and the reinvestment of principal from matured investments, net of estimated credit losses. Costs include the value of the tax relief granted the insurance companies and the annual costs of operating the Insurance Initiatives.

The costs and benefits have been discounted using a 7.5 percent discount rate. The investments from the Insurance Initiatives are expected to yield between 6.0 percent and 7.5 percent. Seven-and-a-half percent represents the highest rate, which is most conservative, and hence has been used as the discount rate.

The NPV of the program costs is $204.0 million. The NPV of the program benefits is $268.8 million. Table 7 shows the NPV calculation for the program benefits and costs.

Once the net value of the program costs and programs benefits are known, the benefit-cost ratio (BCR) and return on investment are calculated. (See table 8.)

Table 5. Benefits.

Funds for Investment in Community Development

Year	Insurance Co. Contributions	Credit Loss	Return of Principal	Available for Investment
1	$36,248,800	$0		$36,248,800
2	36,248,800	−195,381	$0	36,053,419
3	36,317,600	−389,709	0	35,927,891
4	36,348,800	−583,360	0	35,765,440
5	36,348,800	−776,136	0	35,572,664
6	0	−967,873	22,446,027	21,478,154
7	0	−962,656	22,325,043	21,362,387
8	0	−957,467	22,204,711	21,247,244
9	0	−952,306	22,085,027	21,132,721
10	0	−947,173	21,965,989	21,018,816
11	0	−942,068	21,847,592	20,905,524
12	0	−936,990	21,729,834	20,792,843
13	0	−931,940	21,612,710	20,680,770
14	0	−926,917	21,496,217	20,569,301
15	0	−921,921	21,380,353	20,458,432
16	0	−916,952	21,265,113	20,348,161
17	0	−912,009	21,150,494	20,238,484
18	0	−907,094	21,036,493	20,129,399
19	0	−902,204	20,923,106	20,020,902
20	0	−897,341	40,723,319	0
21	0	−892,505	40,728,156	0
22	0	−668,169	40,952,491	0
23	0	−443,834	41,176,827	0
24	0	−219,499	41,401,162	0
Total	**$181,512,800**	**−$18,151,504**	**$508,450,664**	**$469,951,352**

Table 6. Investment turnover rate.

Total amount invested over 20 years	$469,951,352
Initial insurance company contributions	$181,512,800
Turnover rate =	$\dfrac{\text{Total Invested}}{\text{Initial Contributions}}$
Turnover rate =	$\dfrac{\$469,951,352}{\$181,512,800}$
Turnover rate =	2.59

The ROI to the Commonwealth of Massachusetts from the passage of this legislation is 31.77 percent. This ROI calculation was performed using conservative estimates of both benefits and costs.

It appears that the full benefits anticipated by the legislature when they passed this legislation will not be realized. Instead, benefits will be a smaller amount. This smaller program amount has been used in the ROI calculation.

Table 7. Net present value of costs and benefits.

Year	Total Annual Cost	NPV of Annual Cost at 7.5%	Funds Available for Investment	NPV of Available Funds at 7.5%
1	$48,988,000	$45,570,233	$36,248,800	$33,719,814
2	48,717,500	42,156,842	36,053,419	31,198,199
3	48,735,438	39,230,106	35,927,891	28,920,536
4	48,753,823	36,506,889	35,765,440	26,781,180
5	48,772,669	33,973,024	35,572,664	24,778,446
6	791,986	513,176	21,478,154	13,917,017
7	811,785	489,308	21,362,387	12,876,283
8	832,080	466,549	21,247,244	11,913,377
9	852,882	444,849	21,132,721	11,022,478
10	874,204	424,159	21,018,816	10,198,202
11	896,059	404,430	20,905,524	9,435,566
12	918,461	385,620	20,792,843	8,729,961
13	941,422	367,684	20,680,770	8,077,122
14	964,958	350,582	20,569,301	7,473,104
15	989,082	334,276	20,458,432	6,914,255
16	1,013,809	318,728	20,348,161	6,397,197
17	1,039,154	303,904	20,238,484	5,918,806
18	1,065,133	289,769	20,129,399	5,476,189
19	1,091,761	276,291	20,020,902	5,066,672
20	1,119,055	263,440	0	0
21	1,147,032	251,187	0	0
22	1,175,707	239,504	0	0
23	1,205,100	228,364	0	0
24	1,235,227	217,743	0	0
	NPV =	$204,006,657	NPV =	$268,814,404

Likewise, a conservative estimate of program costs has been used. First, there were several estimates of costs of the tax relief to state. Program costs have been calculated using the higher of these estimates. Second, because the insurance industry has not invested in PCI at the anticipated levels, the tax relief will not be as costly to the state as originally anticipated; however, program costs continue to include the costs estimates for tax relief. (See table 9.)

Table 8. Benefit-cost (BCR) ratio.

Program Benefits	$268,814,404
Program Costs	$204,006,657
BCR =	$\dfrac{\text{Program Benefits}}{\text{Program Costs}}$
BCR =	$\dfrac{\$268,814,404}{\$204,006,657}$
BCR =	1.32

Table 9. Return on investment (ROI).

Program Benefits	$268,814,404
Program Costs	$204,006,657
Net Program Benefits	$64,807,747
ROI (%) =	$\dfrac{\text{Net Program Benefits}}{\text{Program Costs}}$
ROI (%) =	$\dfrac{\$64,807,747}{\$204,006,657}$
ROI (%) =	31.77%

Intangible Benefits

In addition to the financial benefits described above, the passage of this community investment act by the Massachusetts legislature has generated some benefits that could not be quantified and included in the ROI calculation. These are known as intangible benefits.

The first intangible benefit is improved relations between the insurance industry and the community development groups. During most of the 1990s the relationship between these groups was characterized by a degree of distrust. In spite of the success of MCRC, the insurance industry was not actively and consistently investing in community development in Massachusetts. The insurance companies had the impression that community development projects were bad investments. The community development groups felt that the insurance companies were happy to take premium dollars from a community, but that they wanted no part of investing in those communities.

The creation of the Insurance Initiatives and the process by which these initiatives were created has changed that. The life insurance companies formed a task force to study community development and community development organizations. One of the outcomes of this task force was an understanding of community development organizations on the part of the insurance companies and an understanding that community development investments did not have to be bad investments. Sound community development investments could be made, and in fact were routinely made by many of the community development lending institutions.

The process of negotiating the legislation also improved the relationship between the groups. In order to get to consensus, each group—the legislature, the community groups, and the insurance companies—had to understand the particular issues affecting the other groups. With this understanding came an improved relationship.

A second intangible benefit was that additional funds were available for community development investment in Massachusetts. One of the financing gaps identified by the life insurance company investment task force was the lack of funds for longer-term loans. A part of the investments from the Insurance Initiatives are for longer-term loans. Additionally, the Insurance Initiatives have invested some of their funds into the loan funds of Massachusetts-based community development lending institutions. That has served to provide additional loan capital to these institutions, strengthening their financial position, and has improved the relationship between these institutions and the insurance industry.

Finally, with this legislation, Massachusetts has provided a model for effective community investment on the part of insurance companies.

Communication Process

This is the first-of-its-kind legislation in the United States. As a result, it has received considerable attention and press coverage. The local Boston press provided extensive coverage of the legislation as it was being negotiated with the legislature and as it became law. The press has continued to cover the Insurance Initiatives over the first years of their existence. This legislation has also been discussed in two articles in journals published by Federal Home Loan Bank of Boston. These journals target banking and investment professionals and are distributed nationally. The articles are also available online.

Additionally, the Insurance Initiatives have held outreach and information meetings throughout the state, and they are required to distribute their investments geographically throughout Massachusetts. One of the criticisms of MCRC had been the concentration of its investments in the Boston area. The purpose of these meetings is to ensure that information regarding the legislation and the Insurance Initiatives is given to community development groups throughout the state.

The Massachusetts Association of Community Development Corporations has written by far the most comprehensive reports on the insurance industry and community investment. Their 1996 report, "The Insurance Industry and Low-Income Communities: A Failure to Invest," was widely distributed among legislators and community groups, and started the wave of industry criticism and community support that ultimately led to the passage of the legislation. Their 2000 report, "Insuring the Future of Our Communities: The First Progress Report on the Massachusetts Insurance Industry Investment Initiatives," describes the progress to-date in implementing the Insurance Initiatives and the benefits from the legislation.

Lessons Learned

The Massachusetts experience in granting tax relief for community investment has been a complicated process. What lessons can we take away from this process?

The primary lesson from this process is the importance of consensus and need for effective negotiation to arrive at consensus. This program provides a positive ROI for the state of Massachusetts, provides significant benefits for the insurance industry, and provides significant benefits for the community development community. The key to structuring this win-win situation is consensus. The insurance industry had been seeking tax relief throughout the 1990s, but had failed to receive it. The community development groups had been looking to the insurance industry for community development dollars since 1991. These efforts too had failed. The relationships between the insurance industry, community development groups, and the legislature included tension and distrust.

These relationships began to change in 1997 when the life insurance companies convened the community development investment task force and continued throughout the negotiation process and through the passage of the legislation in 1998. The linking of community development investment and tax relief was a critical step in creating a win-win situation.

The initial insurance industry community investment bills proposed to the legislature were copies of the bank community investment legislation. The insurance industry felt that these bills did not accurately reflect their unique investment practices, nor did the bills fit within the legal and regulatory structure of an insurance company. The insurance industry had always felt that the community investment provisions were not appropriate as presented. Through the negotiation process, the insurance companies were able to craft legislation that accommodated their investment and regulatory structure. The community development groups received representation on the boards of the Life Initiative and PCI. The process of creating the legislation included representatives from each constituency. The legislation that was ultimately passed reflected this consensus.

The consensus process is what ultimately allowed the program to be structured and was critical in getting the program structured to match the requirements of each party. Had the negotiation and consensus process been started sooner, years of wasted effort could have been avoided.

The other lesson learned from determining the ROI of this program is that it is difficult to determine the appropriate costs and benefits when a longtime horizon is involved. In this case, the program has a 24-year life expectancy. Costs and benefits do not all occur in the same time period. Initial costs are incurred to achieve long-term benefits. In order to calculate the ROI, the program costs and benefits must all be brought back to the present period. This requires that assumptions be made. Care must be taken when making these assumptions, or incorrect or overstated program costs and benefits could be determined. In this case, the program costs and benefits have been brought back to the present period using a net present value calculation, which is a standard method for this purpose. Costs and benefits have been analyzed several different ways, and the most conservative results have been used in the ROI calculation. The process to determine these conservative results requires a complete analysis of the data under differing scenarios. Thoroughness in data analysis is critical to the ROI process.

Questions for Discussion

1. Discuss the NPV assumptions. Would you change any of the NPV assumptions? Which ones? Why?

2. The costs and benefits of this program have been analyzed over the 24-year life. Is this appropriate? If not, what time horizon would you use?

3. Because the Property/Casualty Initiative is not expected to be fully funded and the full tax benefits are not expected to be received by the property/casualty insurance companies, is it still appropriate to include the full cost of tax relief in the calculation of program costs, or should a different number be used? Discuss.

4. What would the ROI be if the cost of tax relief were based on the amount actually contributed to the Insurance Initiatives rather than the full $200 million expected contribution?

5. How important was the linking of community investment and insurance industry tax relief? Could this program have been effectively implemented without this link?

6. Discuss the importance of the negotiation and consensus building process in creating the Insurance Initiatives.

7. Is the model for community development investment developed here applicable in other states? Why? Does tax relief have to be part of the model, or would the model be transportable without tax relief?

The Author

William Hettinger is president and founder of The Wyndham Financial Group, Ltd., an economic development and community development consulting organization. He is an experienced community and economic development professional with more than 20 years' diverse experience in the for-profit and nonprofit sectors. He has extensive experience in real estate, affordable housing development, and community development programs. Prior to Wyndham Financial, he held senior positions with Aetna Inc., Coopers & Lybrand, The MassMutual Financial Group, and Co-op Initiatives, Inc. During the development of the Life Initiative, he served as a member of the life insurance company investment task force.

Further Resources

Browning, L. (August 11, 1998). "Wait Is Over for In-State Insurers." *The Boston Globe.*

Callahan, T. (February 13, 1997). "Now Is the Time for Insurance Companies to Invest in Poor Communities." *The Boston Globe.*

Commonwealth of Massachusetts. (1998). Chapter 259 of the Acts of 1998, "An Act Insuring Community Investment and the Equitable Taxation of Insurance Companies in Massachusetts." Boston.

Economic Innovation International. (May 1997). "Community Investment Preliminary Market Assessment and Range of Investment Options." Report to the Life Insurance Association of Massachusetts and the Life Insurance Companies of Massachusetts. Boston.

Luquetta, A.C. (Winter 2001). "Productive Partnerships: A Progress Report on Insurance Industry Investors." *Communities and Banking.*

Massachusetts Association of Community Development Corporations. (October 1996). "The Insurance Industry and Low-Income Communities: A Failure to Invest." Boston.

Massachusetts Association of Community Development Corporations. (November 2000). "Insuring the Future of Our Communities: The First Progress Report on the Massachusetts Insurance Industry Investment Initiatives." Boston.

Wilmsen, S. (August 1, xxxx). "Agreement Clears Way for Passage of Tax Cut for Insurance Companies." *The Boston Globe.*

Source: P.P. Phillips, ed. (2002). *In Action: Measuring ROI in the Public Sector.* Alexandria, VA: ASTD Press.